797,885 Books
are available to read at

Forgotten Books

www.ForgottenBooks.com

Forgotten Books' App
Available for mobile, tablet & eReader

ISBN 978-0-243-16365-6
PIBN 10627433

This book is a reproduction of an important historical work. Forgotten Books uses state-of-the-art technology to digitally reconstruct the work, preserving the original format whilst repairing imperfections present in the aged copy. In rare cases, an imperfection in the original, such as a blemish or missing page, may be replicated in our edition. We do, however, repair the vast majority of imperfections successfully; any imperfections that remain are intentionally left to preserve the state of such historical works.

Forgotten Books is a registered trademark of FB &c Ltd.
Copyright © 2017 FB &c Ltd.
FB &c Ltd, Dalton House, 60 Windsor Avenue, London, SW19 2RR.
Company number 08720141. Registered in England and Wales.

For support please visit www.forgottenbooks.com

1 MONTH OF FREE READING

at

www.ForgottenBooks.com

By purchasing this book you are eligible for one month membership to ForgottenBooks.com, giving you unlimited access to our entire collection of over 700,000 titles via our web site and mobile apps.

To claim your free month visit: www.forgottenbooks.com/free627433

* Offer is valid for 45 days from date of purchase. Terms and conditions apply.

English
Français
Deutsche
Italiano
Español
Português

www.forgottenbooks.com

Mythology Photography **Fiction**
Fishing Christianity **Art** Cooking
Essays Buddhism Freemasonry
Medicine **Biology** Music **Ancient Egypt** Evolution Carpentry Physics
Dance Geology **Mathematics** Fitness
Shakespeare **Folklore** Yoga Marketing
Confidence Immortality Biographies
Poetry **Psychology** Witchcraft
Electronics Chemistry History **Law**
Accounting **Philosophy** Anthropology
Alchemy Drama Quantum Mechanics
Atheism Sexual Health **Ancient History**
Entrepreneurship Languages Sport
Paleontology Needlework Islam
Metaphysics Investment Archaeology
Parenting Statistics Criminology
Motivational

CHAIRMAN.

FROM 1881.

ELLIOTT AND FRY.　　BAKER STREET, LONDON, W.

Annals
of

1834 1884

Lloyds Register.

Annals of

1834 · LLOYD'S REGISTER OF SHIPPING · LONDON · 1884

Lloyd's Register.

Annals of Lloyd's Register

BEING

A SKETCH

OF THE

ORIGIN, CONSTITUTION, AND PROGRESS

OF

LLOYD'S REGISTER

OF

BRITISH & FOREIGN SHIPPING.

LONDON.

MDCCCLXXXIV.

WYMAN AND SONS, PRINTERS,
GREAT QUEEN STREET, LINCOLN'S-INN FIELDS,
LONDON W.C.

THE CHAIRMAN AND COMMITTEE

OF

Lloyd's Register of British & Foreign Shipping,

UPON THIS,

THE FIFTIETH ANNIVERSARY OF THE FOUNDATION

OF THE SOCIETY,

THINK THE OCCASION A FITTING ONE TO PRESENT TO EACH

SUBSCRIBER, THIS SHORT OUTLINE OF THE ORIGIN AND

PROGRESS OF THE INSTITUTION,—IN THE HOPE

THAT ITS PERUSAL MAY PROVE OF INTEREST

TO ALL CONNECTED WITH SHIPPING.

2, WHITE LION COURT,
   CORNHILL, LONDON,
      30*th October*, 1884.

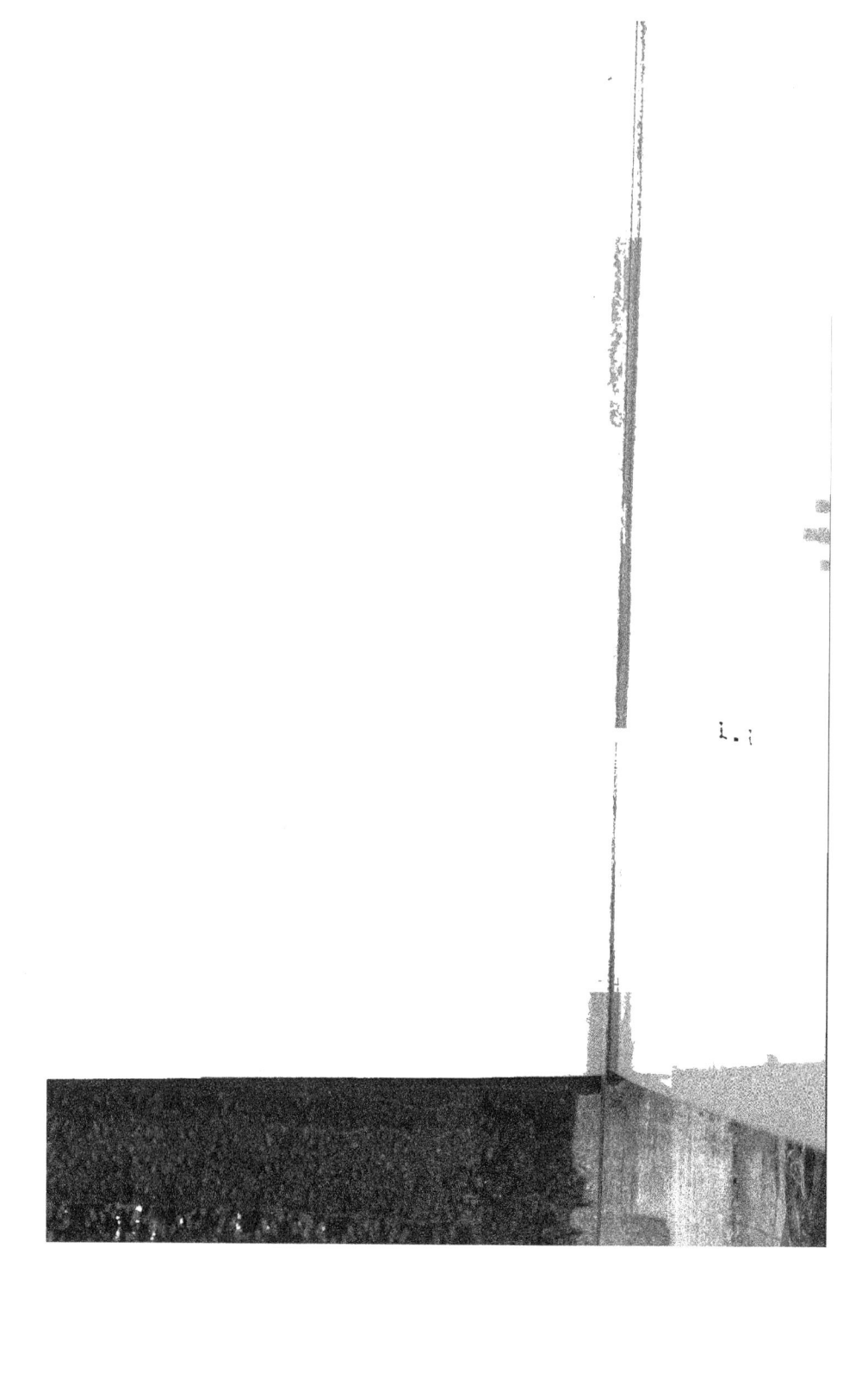

TABLE OF CONTENTS.

CHAPTER I.

Early History of Classification.—Marine Insurance.—Lloyd's Coffee-house.—Ships' Lists.—Oldest Shipping Registers.—Books dated 1764-65-66, 1768-69, and 1775-76 ... 1

CHAPTER II.

Constitution and Working of Underwriters' Register or Green Book.—Surveyors.—Members of Committee.—Symbols and Rules of Classification.—Records in Register Book ... 10

CHAPTER III.

Shipowners' Register or Red Book.—Explanations of their Plan.—Criticisms on Green Book.—Symbols of Classification in Red Book 17

CHAPTER IV.

Subscribers to the two Books.—Symbols of Classification in Green Book re-altered.—Amount of Subscription.—Number of Vessels in the two Books.—Notation of Chain Cables.—Records of Early Steamers.—Early Steam Navigation.—Curious Records.—Shipbuilding Practices ... 23

CHAPTER V.

Rival Registers.—Expressions of Dissatisfaction.—Mr. John Marshall.—His advocacy of Radical Changes in Systems of Classing.—Arguments adduced.—Inquiry demanded.—Committee of Inquiry appointed 29

CHAPTER VI.

Committee of Inquiry. — Their Report. — Suggestions and Financial Plans for Establishment of National Registry.—Collapse of the Movement 35

CHAPTER VII.

Decay of two Registers.—Special Committee of Lloyd's.—Proposed Fusion of the two Books.—Outline of proposed Constitution. — Conference. — Provisional Committee formed.—Proposed Rules and Regulations.—Financial Plans.—First Edition of "Lloyd's Register of British and Foreign Shipping" produced. — Permanent Committee appointed 43

CHAPTER VIII.

Composition of Permanent Committee.—Number and size of Ships in Mercantile Marine in 1834.—Early Rules for Shipbuilding.—Restoration of Vessels to the A Character.—Early Machinery Surveys.—Staff of Surveyors in 1834. — Shipwright and Nautical Surveyors. — Continuation Surveys—Tables for Wood Materials 53

CHAPTER IX.

Society now fully established. — Classification upon a proper Basis.—Application from Outports for more enlarged Representation.—Especially from Liverpool.—Establishment of a Liverpool Register.—Proposed Amalgamation with Lloyd's Register.—Amalgamation effected 64

CHAPTER X.

Excellence of New Rules for Construction and Classification of Ships.—Commercial Depression.—Financial Condition of Society.—Report of Select Committee of House of Commons.—Growth of the Society.—Report of General Shipowners' Society.—Public Opinion regarding the Register.—Number of Vessels Classed per Annum 69

CHAPTER XI.

Iron Ships.—Surveyors' Reports on Iron Shipbuilding.—Iron Rules of 1854.—Rules for Survey of Iron Ships.—Mr. Ritchie on the Society's Operations.—Survey of Iron Steamers 75

CHAPTER XII.

Corrosion of Iron Ships.—Experiments in sheathing them.—Composite Ships.—Preparation of Rules for building them 83

CHAPTER XIII.

Applications from the Provinces in 1863 for share in Management.—Liverpool Proposals.—Extension of the Committee.—Outport Members added.—Representation of Shipbuilders not allowed.—Underwriters' Registry for Iron Vessels.—Proposals for Amalgamation discussed.—Finally rejected.—Liverpool Committee of Lloyd's Register.—Enlarged Powers 87

CHAPTER XIV.

Revision of Rules for Iron Ships in 1863.—Reports of Shipbuilders and Surveying Staff.—Objections to Old System of classifying Iron Ships.—New Symbols adopted.—Periodical Surveys for Iron Ships.—Amendments in Tables of Scantlings.—Revision of Iron Rules in 1870.—Mr. Waymouth's Proposals.—Dimensions adopted in lieu of Tonnage as a basis for Scantlings.—New Symbols 94

CHAPTER XV.

Alteration in Rules for Wood Ships in 1857.—Special Survey Mark ✠ instituted.—Classes for Foreign-built Ships.—Diagonal Doubling.—Alteration in Rules for Wood Ships in 1870.—Salting.—Mixed Material Rule.—Improved Classes to Wood Materials.—Still further improved in 1878.—Defective Equipment 100

CHAPTER XVI.

Surveyors abroad.—North American Timber and Shipbuilding.—Appointment of Surveyors for Canada; also to Holland and Belgium, &c.—Surveyors appointed for Shanghai; also ports in Italy and Austria.—Mr. Waymouth's visit to Genoa.—Present number of Foreign Surveyors 105

CHAPTER XVII.

Equipment Rules in 1834.—Supplemented in 1846.—Testing of Chains.—Rules of 1853.—Table 22 issued.—Equipment Rules of 1862.—Poplar Proving House: its establishment and close.—More stringent Requirements in 1863.—Chain and Anchors Act of 1871.—Proving Houses now under Control of the Society 109

CHAPTER XVIII.

Rules for Survey of Machinery in 1834.—Resolutions of the Committee in 1873.—Engineer Surveyors appointed.—Dangerous arrangements of Pipes and Sea-cocks.—Surveyors' Reports.—Machinery Rules.—Extent of Machinery Surveys 112

CHAPTER XIX.

Manufacture of Steel in 1860.—Steel Shipbuilding in 1862, 1864, and 1866.—Steel tests in 1867.—Bessemer and Siemens-Martin Processes.—Steel "resurrection" in 1877.—Investigations by Society's Officers.—Its use for Ships and Boilers.—Tonnage of Steel Shipping.—Steel Castings.—Inspection of Forgings 118

CHAPTER XX.

Royal School of Naval Architecture.—Royal Naval College.—Private Students.—Grant for Scholarship.—Conditions of Competition 126

CHAPTER XXI.

Classification of Yachts undertaken.—Yacht Register instituted.—Its Growth.—Special Classes for Fishing Vessels   128

CHAPTER XXII.

Draught of Water in Early Register Books.—Awning-deck Vessels.—Their Load-line.—Committee's decision challenged.—Judgment of Court of Law thereon.—Spar-deck Vessels.—Board of Trade detention of Overladen Vessels.—Action of Committee in regard to Load-line Question.—Tables of Freeboard   130

CHAPTER XXIII.

Representation of Outports on Committee.—Proposed extension.—Sub-Committee appointed.—Decision of General Committee.—Present Constitution of Committee...   ...   137

CHAPTER XXIV.

Pensions to Society's Officers.—Insurance Scheme.—Mr. Waymouth's suggestions on the subject.—Pension Scheme adopted by the Committee   140

CHAPTER XXV.

The present Register Book.—Comparison with that of 1834.—Recent Additions.—Number of Subscribers now; also in 1834.—Comparative Tonnages at the two dates.—The Posting of Alterations in the Book   142

CHAPTER XXVI.

Personal.—Mr. Thomas Chapman.—Mr. W. H. Tindall.—List of Chairmen, Deputy-Chairmen, and Chairmen of

Sub-Committees of Classification, from 1834 to 1884.—Early Members of Committee.—Early Officers.—Principal Officers to present time.—Confidence of Government in Society's Officials.—Royal Commissions, &c., on which Society has been represented 145

CHAPTER XXVII.

Conclusion 155

Committee of Management 159
List of Surveyors... 162
Colonial and Foreign Surveyors 164

Annals of Lloyd's Register.

CHAPTER I.

THE early history of the Classification of Ships is veiled in much obscurity. The first recorded attempt to establish anything like an organised Registry dates back no farther than last century, although it admits of little doubt that the classification of merchant shipping in a more or less imperfect form existed long before—if, indeed, it was not contemporaneous with the business of Marine Insurance.

Of the remote beginning of Marine Insurance, with which the subject of classification is so closely allied, little is known. All the best authorities, however, consider that, in some form or other, it was coëval with maritime commerce itself, which goes back to antiquity.

The Phœnicians, the great trading nation of old,

the Greeks, and other ancient peoples, were all, we are told, in the habit of guarding themselves against some of the risks of maritime enterprise by various systems of insurance, whether by means of loans or of mutual guarantees. " Nautical Insurance," as Gibbon terms it, was so common with the Romans, that we find it made the subject of a special provision in one of the Justinian Laws, dated A.D. 533, which, whilst restricting the legal rate of usury to 6 per cent., made special exemption in favour of this "perilous adventure." Coming down to the Middle Ages, we find Marine Insurance carried on regularly in the Italian Republics,—which even went so far as to regulate by law the depth beyond which each vessel should not be loaded,—while operations of this nature were then becoming not unusual in England.

With the practice of insuring ships and their cargoes against sea risk there would naturally arise the necessity of adopting means to ascertain whether the vessels were seaworthy, and to have the relative qualities of ships in this respect classified and recorded in some manner convenient to persons interested in shipping.

The Merchant would not be willing to employ, nor the Underwriter to insure, a ship, without first acquainting himself with her fitness for the carriage of merchandise across the seas. To employ an expert to inspect and report upon every ship when proposed for insurance would only be practicable when few ships existed, and when the business of marine insurance was in its infancy. With the growth of the mercantile marine would grow the demand for a shipping register—not a list of the ships merely, but a record of their size, and of their condition and qualities at specified dates. With such a list before them, the parties interested in a vessel,— the Merchant desirous of securing a safe conveyance for his goods, or the Underwriter willing to insure the risks of the voyage,—could form some reasonable idea of her capabilities without going personally to see her. It is thus evident that a maritime country like England, whose

> Argosies with portly sail,
> Like signiors and rich burghers on the flood,

have long been known in all parts of the world, must have possessed at an early date some such record of the seagoing vessels upon which insurances would be effected.

It appears, indeed, from the researches of the late Mr. Frederick Martin, that accounts of this nature, termed "Ships' Lists," were kept for their own guidance by the early frequenters of Lloyd's Coffeehouse. This establishment, the earliest notice of which occurs in the shape of an advertisement in the *London Gazette* of the 18th February, 1668, was situated first in Tower Street, and from 1692 onward in Lombard Street, at the corner of Abchurch Lane. It was owned by a Mr. Edward Lloyd, under whose able management it became the great resort for all persons connected with shipping, gradually developing into the head-quarters of maritime business, and especially of marine insurance.

That the house was well known is shown by the fact of its having formed the subject of a paper by Steele in the *Tatler* of 1710, and of another by Addison in the *Spectator* of the following year; while it is referred to in *The Wealthy Shopkeeper*, a poem published some ten years earlier, in the following terms:—

> Now to Lloyd's Coffee-house ; he never fails
> To read the letters and attend the sales.

Lloyd seems to have been a man of unusual ability and enterprise. He it was who started that system of shipping intelligence which, under the direction of the great Marine Insurance Corporation of " Lloyd's," has grown to be one of the most extensive and most perfect organisations in the world of commerce. He established and conducted newspapers at a time when journalistic enterprise was in its infancy and the freedom of the press was unknown. His first venture was a shipping and commercial chronicle called *Lloyd's News*, which, begun in September, 1696, and issued three times a week, was brought to a premature end in the following February, in consequence of the Government having taken offence at some trifling allusion to the proceedings of the House of Lords. This paper, however, was the forerunner of the world-famous *Lloyd's List*, which was commenced in 1726, and has continued to the present day. It is thus able to claim the distinction of being, with the sole exception of the official *London Gazette*, the oldest newspaper now in existence.

At Lloyd's Coffee-house, also, if not by Lloyd himself, were started those Ships' Lists already alluded to, containing the germs of *The Register of Shipping* which sprang into public existence at some period during last century, and which, besides being the first English Classification Society of which there is any record, is the parent of all other Shipping Registries now in existence. These Lists, which were written by hand, contained an account of vessels which the Underwriters who met at Lloyd's Coffee-house were likely to have offered to them for insurance. They were doubtless, in the first instance, and probably for some considerable time, passed from hand to hand, much in the same way as the written news-letters of the period. They were most probably first put into type and circulated for the use of subscribers in the form of a printed Register about 1726, the year that witnessed the establishment of *Lloyd's List*. No early copies of such a work, however, appear to be now in existence; any which may have been preserved until that time having, it is supposed, been destroyed in the fire which laid the Royal Exchange in ashes in 1838.

In 1770, the principal Underwriters and Brokers who had for so long made the Coffee-house their meeting-place, found it desirable to form themselves into an association held together by a system of membership, and to remove from Lombard Street. Their first place of meeting was in Pope's Head Alley whence they went a few years later to the Royal Exchange, there to set up on a " permanent footing the great institution which has flourished ever since on the same spot, growing from generation to generation," and making the name of Lloyd's a "household word all over the world."

The oldest copy of a Register of Shipping in the library of Lloyd's Register Office,—indeed, as far as can be ascertained after diligent search, the oldest copy of any book of the kind at present in existence,—bears the date of 1764-65-66, for which period it was evidently current. It is of an oblong form, differing in this respect from all the succeeding volumes, and its singed edges bear evidence of having passed through the flames.

A specimen page of this book, reproduced on the opposite side, shows that the information which it contained was of a very complete nature. It comprised the former and present names of the vessels, those of the owners and masters, the ports between which the vessels traded, the tonnage, the number of their crew and of the guns they carried, the port and year of build; together with the classification printed in the column indicating the year in which the vessels were respectively surveyed, the column headed "66," left blank at publication, being intended to receive the latest alterations in writing. Further particulars were added in the column headed "Guns" in the shape of notations descriptive of the vessels, such as "Sd," single deck, "SdB," single deck with tier of beams, "3 Decks," "Dbld," &c.

The vessels recorded in this volume are for the most part. of very small size; but several are to be found of four, five, and six hundred tons, and there are two ships of eight and one of no less than nine hundred tons.

Formr	Present	Master	Port	To Port	Tons	Guns	M	Built & Year	Owners	64	65	66
W	Walton	Wm. Stone / Sam. Box	Lond.	Dublin	50	S d S L	5	Harw. 1753	Wm. Stone	I M		
	Ward	Alex. Murray		Bermudas	120 s	S D b B	10	Pl. 55 r. 64	Ward	E M	out	out
	Warren	T Vickerman		Nave	600 s	W	30	River R. 46	Vickerman	E M	E M	
D. Cumb.	Wareham	J. Thompson		Ireland	50	S D S L	5	Fren. R. 63	J. Thompson	E M		
	Watsl Trade	Jof. Norman	Liverp.	Waterford	40		6	British 56	Wallace & C.	E M		
	Wellbeloved	John Snow	Lond.	Guernsey	40	S d	5	French 58	Lugove			E M
	Wesn Gally	R. Knowler		Port	160		10	River 53	J. Bailey	E M	E M	
Alexander	Westmorelᵈ	W. Hore		Jamaica	250	8	4	Plantation 55	Ed. Hore	E M	E M	
	Westmorelᵈ	Wm. Luce		New York	140		10	63	Jo. Chetwood	A G	A G	A M
	Wetherel	Dd. Mayin		St. Christo	200		12	63	Wm. Pritty	E M	E M	cut
Elizabeth	Weymouth	W. Bartlitt		Greenland	280	dbled	36	French 56	Enderby out			IM
Lost	WheelFortᵉ	Rd. Maneſty	Liverp.	Barbadoes	180 s		16	French 54	Tho. Weſten			
	Whitehaven	Philipfon		Colerain	50 s	S d S L	3	British 50	Okill & Irish	E M	K M	
	Wilhelmus	Ad. Janfen	Lond.	Hamburgh	240		12	Hamb. 50	Wilhelmus	E M	E M	E M
	William	W. Burckett		Ostend	90	S d B	7	River 37	W. Burchett	E M	E M	
	William	Th. Harbutt		Dieppe	150	S d B	0	Scarbor. 59	T. Harbutt			O M
	William	J. Brokley	Topſh.	Bilboa	50	SD B	6	Barnstable	Tho. Brook			
S. Andrew	William	T. Wheele	Lond.	Jamaica	200 s	6 S d b 4	16	Liverpool	Parkinſn &C.	E M	E M	
	William	J. Forſter.	Hull	Dublin	150 s	S d	9	French	Joel Foster		O M	
	William	Rt. Anderfon	Lond.	Mahone	100 s	S d b B	8	Plantatt. 56	Twedale &C	E M	E M	
	William	Chr. Spurier	Pool	Waterford	70	B	7	French 50	W. Spurier	E M	E M	I M
	William	Abf. Tavern		Carolina	70	S N	8	Bristol 53	P. Jolliff	E M	E M	P E
	William	W. Gilchrist	Liverp.	Bally Castle	30	S L	8	British 63	Glasgow	A G	A G	
	William	Pat. Shaw		Colerain	40		3	54		E M	E M	

1768 69 70 71

an Sk	L. Beckman	50	Friesnd	59	Raasper, Brem	a2 67	Lo. Bremen	
orse Sp	Daniel Hack	30 SD	Chichr	60	Capt. prt Owr		a2 11 Chichr Dub	
l S	Jos. Miller	200	Amer.	64	Mr. Lester	a1	Pool N York	
S d	Robert King	450 SDB	Whitby	50	Jn Yeaming's	b2 3	a2 Lon. Memel	ag // Mbngl 3
Bg	Simd Smith	90 SD	Yarmth	64	N. Simmonds	a1 8	a2 Yar. Malaga	a Ostend Var 3
S s f Wales	Mos. Henry	250	London	51	Mr Henry, Lo	a2	b2 Lo. Antigu 11	ag back
S s	Leod Brooks	300	London	49	Ward, Wtby	a2	Lon. Maryld	
ary S s n	Wm Innis	300	Hull	61	Ward, Wtby	a1	a2 10 Petersb. Lon	ag Jo. Cot Sea 2
ale Bg	Jhn Johnson	140 SDB	Yarmth	60	G. Radsdale		a2 11 Scheedm Lo	
ow S	PW Westcot	220	Amer.	63	Lane & Co.	a2 66	Lon. Carol.	
S	Jms Caldwel	150 SDB	Amer.	61	Benson & Co.	b2	Liv. N. York	
Bg	Jm Gregory	90	Amer.	65	Jms Whittel	a1 3	a1 Pool N'flang	q back 2
Sp	John Davis	40	S'thmtn	52	Mr. Gardner	a2 5	a2 Guernsey Lo	ag 7
Sr	James Major	120 SD	Amer.	63	Cap. prt Owr	a2	Guernsey Lo	
Bg	G. Hamiltn	50 SD	Scotlnd	65	to Scotland		b1 4 Glasgw Du	
& Margt Sp	Jeckling	60 SDB	Wells	63	Ral. Forster	a2	Lyn Gottnb.	
ate Sp	S. Sparrow	36	River	56	Mr Nightngl	a2 67	Lo. Madeira	
lph S	Rbt Walker	250 len.	London 61	53	Lancastr & Co	a2 9	a2 Lon. Virgin 11	a2 1 aq // 2
S s	Jn Harbison	300	Stocktn	53	Webster & Co	a2 3	a2 Jamai. Lon	a2
S s	Dd Tuothy	150 67	Liverpl reb	54 67	Clemens & Co	b2	b2 Liv. Afr. &c 11	b2 1
s	Dan. Jacksn	140	Plantat.	59	Dav. Kenyon	2 66	Liv. B'bdoes	
S d	Isr. Hunter	350 SDB	British thro' rep.	48 65	Tho. Hunter	a2	a2 Petersb. Lon 11	ag // g
S	Ste. Blundell	200	Poole	66	Kemp & Cap.	a1 4	a1 Pool N'flang	a ay baglara 2
Bg	Rbt Forsyth	120	Maryld new Sides.	62	to Maryland	a2 67	Dub. Maryl.	

face p 7

The classes assigned to the vessels were designated by the letters A, E, I, O, and U, which referred to the vessels' hulls, while the letters G, M, and B,—meaning "good," "middling," and "bad,'—' related to the equipment. Thus the class AG would denote a first-class ship with a good outfit, while UB would be the designation given to a ship of the lowest class, and with a bad outfit.

The title-page and the front pages of this book are wanting, but it appears from the last page that the work was "Printed by W. Richardson and S. Clark, in Fleet Street," the firm which in all probability succeeded to the business of Richardson the novelist, who, it is well known, had a printing establishment in this street some years before the date of issue of this volume. Judging from the completeness of this edition, it is only reasonable to suppose that the Register must have existed for some considerable time previously.

The next Register, in point of date, preserved in the Office at White Lion Court, is dated 1768–69, columns being left blank for posting by hand particulars for the years 1770–71. This volume differs considerably both in regard to form and arrangement of contents from the book we have just described, as will be seen upon reference to the specimen page given on the other side. In addition to the particulars stated in the earlier Register, this book also contained references to the vessels' rigs, and afforded information of the repairs effected, such as "rep.," "thro' rep.," "great rep.," "well rep.," "good rep.," "reb.," &c.

The most remarkable difference, however, occurs in the symbols of classification. Instead of the capital letters A, E, I, O, and U being employed for designating the several classes, we now find the small letters ᵃ, ᵇ, and ᶜ used for that purpose; while the numerals 1, 2, 3, and 4 are now adopted for the first time in describing the condition of the equipment. For instance, "ᵃ1" in this Register denoted a first-class ship with a first-class equipment, while "ᵇ2" denoted a second-class ship with a second-class equipment. It will thus be seen that between the years 1764 and 1768 a change had been made from "AG" to "ᵃ1" in the direction of the designation "A 1."

The third earliest Register preserved is dated 1775–76, and in arrangement much resembles the preceding one; but in this book the Roman capitals are again employed for the classification of the hull, while the figures 1 and 2 remain for that of the equipment. This volume appears to be the earliest book extant, containing the now familiar class of A 1. It may be observed that in this issue the load-draught of water appears to have been inserted in place of the column formerly appropriated for the number of men in the crew, and the alterations which, in the earlier copies alluded to, had been made with pen and ink, were now posted weekly in type, as at the present time.

The arrangement of the work in subsequent editions remained substantially the same, no alteration being made beyond the occasional introduction of a few more particulars, such as, whether a vessel had a deep waist or a low counter, whether she was American property, what timber was used in her con-

G

1775 76

Gabriel	Sp	JeanLoiſell	50	French.	69	Capt. & Co.	7 Lo Oſtend C.	A. 1 3	F. 1 3
Gale	Sw s	H Jefferſon	200	Whithvn S.rpts, 76	58	Capt. & Co.	14 Virgin.Lo Lo.Tranſprt	E. 1 1	E. 1 2
Gallam Packet	Sp	Wm Smith	40 SD	Scotland		J.Shoolbred	Lo. Seneg 73	I. 1	
		rmmnd	100	Nw York	68	T Lynch & C	11 Tenrif. B.	E. 1 11	—
		Miller	60 SD	Pool	74	Garland &C	10 Po. Spain	A. 1 9	A. 1
	S s 76	et L. Preſton	420	Whitby grp 74	59	Wm Barker	16 Lo. Trſprt	E. 1 9	F. 1 2
—	Bg s	H. Piper	120 SDB	America S.rpts, 76	70	Capt. & Co.	11 IreindWn	A 1 10	E 1 9
Garnet	Bg	Sl Moreton Jn Kay	80 SD	British	66	Ar. Hughes Capt.&Co,	10 Li. Dnkrk	E. 2 2	F. 2 5
Garrit's Town	Sr	G. White	60 SDB	Kinſale	73	Capt. & Co	8 Br Kinſale	A. 1 8	A 1 9
Gatton		W. Money	75 8	River	71		Bombay 2d Voyage		
Gedrel Regina	Dr	J. Lamma C.B.Volkers	100 SD	Stolp	67	J Blackburn	10 Li. Dantz.	A. 2 8	F. 1
GenerlConway Amity's Aſſiſt. S	s & d 74 Bg s	Rd Kitchen R.Thurſt T Kennedy	450 grp70,&lrp 130	Scarbro' Nw York	54 74 56	J Wilkinſon 16 — 6 & 10 New-York	17 Lo.Grnld 4 Pol. Tranſprt 14 Cadiz Br.	E. 1 2 E. 1 74	F. 1 3
— Murray Neptune	Bg s 76	Rt Gill	160 SDB	Nwcaſtle len.65 &trp	57 74	Capt. & Co.	11 Gernſy Lo Lo. G ttnbrg	E. 1 11	E. 1 1
— Payne	S s	Rt Adams	260	Boſton A	71	Lane & Co.	16 Lo.SKitts C.	A. 1 5	A. 1 4
— Thomas Yeoman	74 S s 75	R Littlwort	150	Shorham trp.75		Capt.	11 Lo.	E. 1 5	
— Wolfe	Bg	Hugh Hill	130 SDB	N.Engld	70	Rt Hooper	11 Co Antiga	A. 2 2	F. 2 8
GenrousFriend	Bg	Wm Knox	120	N.Scotia	66	Capt.	Cs Philad. 73	I. 1	
—	S s 73	Rd Nairne	160	N.Engld	71	Capt. & Co.	12 Maryld Lo Lo.Quebec	A. 1 15	A. 1
—	S s & d 67	Jn Simpſon 12 Guns	200 SDB	Scarbro' trp67,NEW	54 70	H. Simpſon & S.rpts 73 &76	14 Lo.Arkngl Co.Tranſprt	E. 1 4	E. 1 5
	nd		200	Piſcat.	73	Lane & Co.	13 Antiga Lo	A. 1 6	A. 1 6
Endeavour —Friends YoungElizabeth72	73 S s Whitway Blair	T. Walton Js	120 230	America lrp.71 Kg's Yrd rb.66, grp.	63 55 71	Capt. & Co. Deacon & Co. s 75	11 Amſtm Lo 14 Lo St Kitts	E. 2 74 E. 1 2	
— Andaluſia	Bg	T. Leeths	120 SDB	Pool	68	Capt.	10 Lo Wtrfrd Lo.Tranſprt	E. 1 11	F. 1 2

face p. 8.

struction, &c. A list of the ships of the Royal Navy and of the East India Company was also introduced.

The front cover and first page of the three earliest books are, unfortunately, missing, but these books contain sufficient internal evidence to show that the two later volumes form part of the series of *The Register of Shipping* founded in 1760, of which there is a very complete collection from 1775 onwards. This Registry was latterly known as the "Underwriters' Register," or the Green Book. As already stated, the earliest volume (dated 1764-65-66) differs from the succeeding books, and this fact has given rise to the supposition that it did not belong to the same series, but was the issue of a rival Register, which was still in existence in 1768-69, when the small letters were in use by the Underwriters' Register, but had disappeared before 1775, leaving its successor free to adopt the capital letters in combination with figures as a designation of class, which has almost ever since been retained.

CHAPTER II.

IN the absence of more complete records than those now in existence, it is difficult to ascertain accurately what were the constitution and practical working of the Registry established in 1760. It is pretty evident, however, from the most reliable sources of information at hand, that the Register was established and supported exclusively by Underwriters for their sole use as " Members of the Society," as the Subscribers were then termed, and that the subscriptions formed the principal, if not, indeed, the only, source of revenue. The work was issued at first biennially, and after a few years annually. Strict rules were adopted and rigidly enforced, with the object of confining the use of the book to Members. Each Subscriber at the end of the year was obliged to deliver up his old book before a new one was issued to him, and at one time, if a book were lost or stolen, the person to whom it belonged was refused another, although willing to pay for it. The volume for 1779–80 contains the following quaint prohibition :—

"COPY of the BY-LAWS relating to the reserving the REGISTER-BOOKS for the Use of the MEMBERS of the SOCIETY only.

"As the interest of the Society is, in the first Instance, greatly hurt by the Custom of shewing the Books, and leaving them at Places where they are but too common, thereby preventing many Underwriters from becoming Members, who, though they reap the Advantages and Benefits in common with them, do not pay their Quota towards the expenses of the Institution, thereby, as much as in them lies, reducing the Members to the Necessity of paying larger Subscriptions."

"XII. It is therefore agreed to by the Society, and every Member thereof, and ordered by them to be a standing Rule and By-law strictly to be observed, that if any Member shall, after the 6th of February, 1773, shew or give his Book to any Person whatever, not a Member of the Society, to read the Description or Character therein of any Ship, or shall read the same to him, or tell him the same after looking in his Book, or lend the said Book to him, such Member shall forfeit the Sum of 5s. 3d., and, for the second Breach of this By-law the Sum of 10s. 6d., for the third Breach thereof the Sum of £1. 1s., and for the fourth (all of them in Manner aforesaid and within the Year) his Book shall not be posted any more, except he pays the Sum of Two Guineas and all former Forfeitures, within Fourteen Days of the Notice he shall receive thereof from the Secretary; or pays the Sum of Five Guineas for a new Book any time thereafter, within the Year, and delivers up his old one."

"XIII. In like Manner, if any Member shall leave his Book at any Place, except where he shall himself appoint constantly to leave the same locked up; and that said Book, by that Means cannot be found for three Days, or shall be found in the Possession of any Person not a Member; such Member shall in like Manner forfeit as before, for the 1st, 2nd, 3rd, and 4th Breach of the said By-law: But if the Book shall be entirely lost, the Forfeit shall be settled by the Committee, and the Member be obliged to pay Five Guineas for a new one."

The front pages of all the older books are missing, but the volume for 1777–78, although without the title-page, contains a "List of the Members of the Society," numbering about a hundred and thirty, and including the most eminent Members of Lloyd's. It seems, from the following announcement printed on the inside of the cover of the volume for 1781–82 (but, unfortunately, partially destroyed by the cutting out of the Subscriber's name), that the Members or Subscribers met occasionally to discuss matters pertaining to the Register.

"At a General Meeting of the Society, on the 12th December last, it was unanimously resolved:

"That Mr. Alexander Stupart be appointed to survey any damage sustained by [Shipping] which is to be repaired in the River of Thames; and [that] Underwriters be desired to employ him in that service [which it is] supposed will be attended with many advantages."

"That the expence of Mr. Stupart's surveys be paid [by the] Society, to be determined annually."

Although this is the first, and, indeed, only reference in any of the early volumes to Surveyors, there can be no doubt that such Officers were employed from a much earlier period, as we find it intimated in a previous book that all ships not surveyed within three years preceding the issue of the volume had been left out. Besides this fact, the occurrence in the 1768–69 Register Book of the records referring to repairs already alluded to seems to point to a supervision being exercised by Officers of the Society upon ships when under repair, even so far back as that date.

In the issue dated 1797-98 appear for the first time the "Names of the Gentlemen who compose the Committee for conducting the Affairs of the Society," numbering eleven, and including Mr. John Julius Angerstein, the Chairman of Lloyd's.

The members of the Committee were:—

John Julius Angerstein,	Geo. Curling,
William Bell,	Wm. Hamilton,
John Bourke,	Robert Hunter,
John Campbell,	Robert Pulsford,
Alex. Champion,	Edward Vaux,
Jacob Wilkinson.	

It is not clear whether the Committee were in existence from the commencement of the Registry, or were appointed just prior to this publication of their names; neither is there anything to show whether the Committee were elected by, and were directly responsible to, the Members or Subscribers, or whether vacancies as they arose were filled up by the Committee from the body of Members. It seems most probable, however, that the Committee were formed prior to the institution of the Registry in 1760, and that they exercised the power of filling up vacancies in their own body. The meetings of the Committee were, it appears, always held at Lloyd's Coffee-house, but the office of the Registry was situated first in Sun Court and subsequently in Castle Court, Birchin Lane.

In the Register Book for 1797-98 a new style of classification was introduced, which, being scarcely equitable in its operation, aroused feelings of considerable dissatisfaction, and ultimately led to the formation of a rival Register. The changes were of two kinds—for not only the conditions of classification, but also the symbols denoting the classes, were altered. The characters assigned were M for the first class, G for the second class, L for the third class, and Z for the lowest class, with the numerals 8 or 4 attached; and the classification appears to have been so altered as to depend entirely upon the place of build and the age of the vessel. Thus, while a vessel built on the Thames would be entitled to continue on the first class for a term of thirteen years, another ship of the same description built at one of the northern ports would be considered eligible for a period of only eight years; while prize ships whose ages were not ascertained could receive no characters whatever—the numeral describing the condition of the equipment and the date of survey being alone inserted in such cases. As regards the latter class of vessel, of which there appears, from records of the period, to have been a considerable number, a note in the Register Book states that, "When the Ages of Prize Vessels cannot be ascertained, FP, SP, or DP is put in the Column for the Age to denote the Nation from whom they have respectively been captured. And, when the Surveyors can ascertain their Age to be less than Three Years, AN is put into the Column for the Age to denote that the Vessel is almost new."

It is interesting to notice the low estimation in which vessels built in the northern ports were held, not only at this time, but for long after. Twenty-five years later considerable evidence was taken by a Joint Committee of Merchants, Shipowners, and Underwriters upon this subject; and, although it was generally admitted by the persons examined that there were no reasons why as good a ship might not be built in a northern port as in the Thames, yet it was the general opinion that usually the London-built ships were worthy of at least a year longer classification than those of Newcastle, Sunderland, &c. Mr. Edward Gibson, a shipbuilder of Hull, in his evidence before this Committee, stated that "ships built on the river Thames are unquestionably better than those built at outports: the London builders obtain better prices, and can therefore afford to build them of a better description. If the same inducements were held out, there is no reason why vessels built at the outports should not be equally good."

To give so great an advantage to London-built ships was evidently a mistake, for by such a regulation shipbuilding enterprise elsewhere was considerably damaged, while at the same time no guarantee was obtained that the favoured builders would continue to produce such superior ships as before. There can be no doubt that then, as now, excellent vessels were built at all parts of the British Islands, and that the first step towards getting a good ship was to pay a good price.

The dissatisfied Shipowners made strong representations on the subject to the Registry Committee, and, failing to obtain the assent of the latter to their views, several of them, in 1799, started *The New Register Book of Shipping*, having offices at No. 22, Change Alley, and afterwards at No. 3, St. Michael's Alley. This work, although bearing on the title-page the statement that it was issued by a "Society of Merchants, Shipowners, and Underwriters," appears to have been in reality managed by Shipowners only, and was commonly known as the "Shipowners' Register," or *Red Book*. The characters assigned by the new Registry were expressed by the vowels A, E, I, and O, with the figures 1, 2, and 3 for the condition of the "materials,"—as the equipment of a vessel was then termed. The new Register Book was a trifle larger than the Underwriters' Book, of which it was, both as regards the particulars it contained and their arrangement, a precise copy. The elder Society appears to have had Surveyors stationed at twenty-four ports in the United Kingdom, viz. :—

Belfast,	Exmouth,	Leith,	Star Cross,
Bristol,	Exeter,	Liverpool,	Teignmouth,
Cork,	Falmouth,	London,	Topsham,
Cowes,	Greenock,	Lynn,	Waterford,
Dartmouth,	Hull,	Poole,	Whitehaven,
Dublin,	Lancaster,	Portsmouth,	Yarmouth.

The Shipowners' Society modified this list slightly in the case of their Book, leaving out Exmouth and Star Cross, and appointing representatives at Newcastle, Plymouth, Sunderland, Shields, Workington, and Whitby, in addition to those at the other twenty-two ports.

CHAPTER III.

AT the date to which we have now come (1799) there were, therefore, two Register Books in operation, known as the Green Book and the Red Book, the former being the Underwriters' and the latter the Shipowners' Register.

The following was the constitution of the committee of the Red Book in 1799:—

John Hill, *Chairman.*

Norrison Coverdale,	Charles Kensington,
Robert Curling,	Thomas King,
Joseph Dowson,	William Leighton,
Thomas Horncastle,	John Lyall,
Ives Hurry,	J. J. Oddy,
Ralph Keddey,	William Sims,
Thomas Keddey,	William Thompson.

The Committee of the Red Book, in an explanation with which they prefaced that volume, mentioned that—

"The Society for conducting the Publication of the New Register Book of Shipping think it necessary to give a general Explanation of their Plan, as well as to state the Motives which induce them to undertake a Work of so much importance.

"It is well known that a Book has, for a long series of years, been annually printed under the direction of a Committee of a Society, formed of Subscribers, for the information of Underwriters; which Book, after a variety of alterations, was at length arranged in a manner that gave general satisfaction; and, having continued above twenty-four years to be the record of the age, burthen, built, quality, and condition of vessels and their materials, marked according to the opinion of skilful and diligent Surveyors (employed by the Society in all the principal ports of the kingdom) *had* become a *Book of Authority*, and, in a great degree, governed the Merchant, the Shipowner, and Underwriter, in their opinions of the quality of Ships for the purpose of freighting goods or insuring, and, consequently, in a great measure regulated their value.

"In the preceding year the Committee of the Society, without consulting the Subscribers at large, made an entire change in this system, so long established and so universally approved, and substituted in its place a plan founded on a principle diametrically opposite and perfectly erroneous.

"Instead of classing the Ships which they gave an account of according to the actual state and condition, ascertained by a careful Surveyor, a new system was adopted of stamping the character of the Ship wholly by her age and the place in which she was built, without any regard to the *manner* in which she was originally constructed, the wear or damage she might have sustained, or the repairs she might from time to time have received, *or even being rebuilt:* thereby at once obviating the necessity of surveying the hulls of vessels, lessening the inducement to build Ships upon principles of strength and durability, and taking away the encouragement to keep them in the best state of repair, that they might maintain their character in the Register Book alluded to."

A list of the classes assigned to vessels built at the several ports was then given, by which it seems that in the Green Book the thirteen-years class was given to ships built in the River Thames, Royal Dockyards, and India. The twelve-years class was assigned to vessels built in certain ports on the south coast of England. Many of the Channel ports, however, were considered capable of producing only ten-year ships; Liverpool and Bristol also being in this list. To vessels built in Scotland, Wales, the north-east ports of England, and some of the east coast ports, only eight years were assigned. French, Dutch, Spanish, Italian, Portuguese, and some German ships were also granted a term of eight years. United States built ships were allowed twelve years when built of the live oak of the Southern States, but otherwise only six years were granted to them. Colonial and fir-built vessels were allowed as little as five, and in some cases only four years; but ships built at Quebec and Bermuda were granted a class of ten years. Upon the expiration of the number of years first assigned on the M letter, a continuation on the G letter, or second class, was given. Vessels classed thirteen years were further allowed seven years on the letter G; those of twelve and ten years obtained five years; and those of eight years were continued for six years; while six-year vessels were allowed another four years, and so on.

The Red Book Committee go on to say in their introductory explanation:—

"No general reasons have been assigned for the new plan; and, as to the distinction of places, imagination is left to its free scope to ascertain what causes make some situations so inferior to others; for instance, why should ships built at Quebec stand in the first class two years longer than vessels built at Hull or the Northern ports of this kingdom, Wales, &c.? and professional men are equally at a loss to conjecture why the Committee have thought proper to class the shipping of some ports in these kingdoms in degrees so much inferior to that of others; not to say anything respecting the relative situations in which ships in foreign ports are placed. On the first appearance of this new system, meetings were held by a numerous body of the shipowners of this city, who came to resolutions, expressing in the strongest manner their disapprobation of the conduct of the Committee of the Society, and amongst other resolutions declared their opinion that it was 'founded in error, and calculated to mislead the judgment of merchants and underwriters, and, if continued, would not only prove of the most injurious consequences to individual shipowners, merchants, and underwriters, but to every branch of trade connected with repairing and refitting vessels; and in a great measure tend to destroy the shipping of the country.'"

After a few further remarks, from which we learn that the Shipowners' Committee, when they sought to point out to the Committee of the *Green Book* the injurious tendency of their system, were refused an interview by the latter, the *Red Book* Committee proceed to indicate the character of their Rules. These are so brief as to occupy but one page of the book, and contain no instructions whatever in regard to the scantlings and construction of ships, but refer only to the place of their build. Singularly enough, after complaining of a similar system, the Shipowners' Committee adopted a method of original classification based almost entirely upon the locality in which the ships were built, but with the important difference that subsequent classification at the expiration of the original class depended upon the condition of repair in which they were found.

Thames-built ships, if built entirely of British oak and well fastened, were classed twelve years, and "country-built" ships, on the same conditions, were classed for ten years. It is scarcely necessary to state in detail the rules of classification adopted in the new Register. It may be sufficient to say that the four classes were, as already mentioned, represented by the letters A, E, I, and O.

The second class, marked E, included all ships kept in perfect repair that appeared on survey to have no defects, and to be completely calculated to carry a dry cargo safely.

The third class, marked I, was composed of ships which, from defect or want of thorough and substantial repair, did not appear upon survey perfectly safe to carry dry goods, though deemed seaworthy for carrying goods not liable to sea damage.

The fourth class, marked O, was composed of vessels out of repair, which were not deemed safe and seaworthy for a foreign voyage.

The numerals 1 and 2 after the letter related to the "ship's materials" or outfit; if well found, the vessel was marked 1, and if indifferently found she was marked 2.

The system of classification adopted by the Committee of the Red Book was also based, although perhaps to a less extent than in the

Green Book, upon the place of build and the age of the vessel. Under the regulations of both Societies, a vessel, upon the expiration of her original class, lapsed to an inferior grade, and no amount of repairs or strengthening would enable her to be again placed upon the A 1 character; while in neither case were there any Rules for the construction and systematic survey of vessels, and the Surveyors were practically uncontrolled in their decisions. In both cases the systems were unsound; and, although the books remained in concurrent circulation until they were merged in the present Society in 1834, their operations appear to have encountered the hostility of a large section of the Shipping community long before that date.

CHAPTER IV.

AT the beginning of the year 1800, the Green Book numbered 233 subscribers, and the Red Book only 125; but during the year the latter received an accession of no less than 76 subscribers, one of whom took twelve books, whereas the Green Book only shows 31 new members during the year. It would thus appear that the Shipowners' Register very quickly gained popularity and strength in the early stage of its existence.

In 1800 the Committee of the Underwriters' Register, or Green Book, influenced, apparently, by the agitation which their altered system of classification had provoked, returned to the use of the former symbols of character, A, E, I, O, and U. In the issue for the same year was also witnessed the introduction for the first time of a title-page to the work, with the inscription "Instituted in 1760." A "Key to the Register Book" was also then inserted, which, however, gave no real explanation of the manner in which a ship was classed. Another alteration observed in this volume is the entry of the age of a vessel in place of the year of build, which was formerly recorded.

The re-appearance in the Green Book of the old signs was not without its effect upon the circulation of its rival. Accordingly, in the following issue, or third edition, of the Red Book, we find a new preface inserted, pointing out that, although at first sight it might appear that the Committee of the other Register had forsaken their new principles, and returned to their original system, yet "it will be found, on inspection, that the new plan is still adhered to, namely, that of giving characters to ships according to their ages and the places where built, without a due regard to the manner in which they were originally built, the repairs they have received, and their actual state and condition."

It is clear, however, upon a careful scrutiny of the Books issued about this period, that the practice of the Underwriters' Register had been altered in at least one particular. According to the Rules current in 1798–99, prize ships and other vessels whose ages could not be ascertained were not eligible to receive any class whatever. But many of the vessels of this description, which were refused characters in that and previous years, appeared in the succeeding editions of the Green Book with classes assigned to them.

From a receipt written upon one of the fly-leaves of the Red Book for 1801, now in the collection at Lloyd's Register Office, it seems that the amount of the subscription for this volume was, from its commencement, eight guineas per annum. It was, doubtless, mainly due to this fact that the Committee of the Underwriters' Register, in 1810 (the fiftieth year of its existence), reduced the price of their Book from twelve to eight guineas.

The vessels classed in the oldest Register Book extant, namely, that dated 1764–65–66, amounted to 4,500. This number went on steadily increasing until it reached 8,271 in 1800, in which year the second edition of the Shipowners' Register contained particulars of 7,754 vessels. During the following twelve months, however, the New Register Committee added a large number of ships to their Book, so that the next issue—that in 1801—comprised even more vessels than were included in the Underwriters' Register, there being 9,145 vessels in the latter and 9,540 in the former volume.

Iron cables would appear to have been introduced about 1813, vessels supplied with them having the words "Iron Cable" noted against their names; and in 1816 the letters "P. I. C." were employed to denote that the cables had been proved. There is, however, a note in the Register for 1824, to the effect that, in the case of vessels fitted with iron cables, and having none of hemp, the figure denoting the quality of the equipment was omitted; but the question had become of such importance in 1828, that full instructions regarding the same were issued to the Surveyors of the Underwriters' Book.

In glancing over the old volumes forming part of the collection of the Underwriters' Register, we are reminded of the fact that, in the early part of the present century, steam navigation was practically unknown.

It is not until 1822 that we find any record of a

steamship in the Register. In the supplement to the Book bearing that date there occurs the entry of a steam packet, appropriately named the *James Watt*, of 294 tons, built at Greenock in 1821, and classed A 1. Although this is noteworthy, as being the first appearance of a steamer in the Register, we learn that for several years previously vessels propelled by steam had gradually come into public notice.

Indeed, as far back as 1736, an invention "for carrying Vessels or Ships out of or into any Harbour, Port, or River, against Wind and Tide, or in a Calm," was patented by a Mr. Jonathan Hulls. His idea, however, does not appear to have been put into execution, although several attempts were made during the following fifty years to build a steamer. No result of any real importance was obtained until 1787, when Mr. William Symington, at the instigation of Mr. Patrick Miller, an Edinburgh banker, fitted a steam-engine on board a large boat in the Forth and Clyde Canal, a trial of which took place and proved highly satisfactory.

The distinction, however, of possessing the first practical steamboat was reserved for Lord Dundas, who, in 1801, had a vessel constructed by Mr. Symington, which he named the *Charlotte Dundas*. This steamer, it is stated, towed two loaded vessels against a strong breeze, along the Forth and Clyde Canal to Port Dundas, a distance of $16\frac{1}{2}$ miles, in six hours. This vessel had to be laid up for several years, in consequence of the fear of the proprietors of the canal that the wash of the boat would injure the banks!

The idea, however, was now fairly started, and in 1811, Henry Bell, of Glasgow, after some years of experimenting, built a steamer, the well-known *Comet*, which carried passengers between ports on the Frith of Clyde. Other steamboats quickly followed, and amongst them one built in London in 1814, which was tried on the canal near Limehouse, the Lord Mayor and other celebrities being on board at the time. Indeed, to such importance had the subject grown in 1817 that a Committee of the House of Commons sat in that year to consider the means of preventing the mischief arising from explosions on board steamboats. As the result of their investigations, regulations were issued which required all steamboats to be registered, and, in the case of passenger-vessels, the boilers—which it was thought necessary to prescribe should be of wrought-iron or copper—were to be submitted to inspection. Each boiler was required to be fitted with two safety-valves, and to be tested to three times the working pressure, which was not to exceed one-sixth the pressure the boiler was calculated to withstand.

It would thus appear that the Committee of the Register Book were far behind the times in admitting steamers to classification; but from the year 1822, when the entry of the *James Watt* was made, the number of classed steam vessels rapidly increased, the Book for 1827 containing 81 steamers, whilst that for 1832 included no fewer than 100. Whatever may have been the Rules which guided the Register in the classification of steamers, they were evidently of a very imperfect nature, containing no provision for the periodical examination of such vessels. It is observed, for instance, that the last-named ship remained classed on the A character without having been surveyed from her entry in 1822 until the year 1830, after which, her term of classification having apparently expired, she disappeared from the Register Book.

Amongst the curious records to be found in some of the Register Books of early date may be mentioned the following:—"s.s.," small scantlings, in the Book for 1812; "sheathed with zinc," in 1820,—this being the first notice of a vessel sheathed with this material; and "sheathed with tanned leather," in 1831.

It further appears that even at this early period it was not unusual for builders of wooden vessels to employ salt to preserve the timbers from dry-rot, even to the extent of boiling them in salt water.

The beneficial effect of salt on timber was sufficiently exemplified in the frames of river craft employed in its conveyance, which, in many cases, after fifty years' service were found as sound as when first built.

Coming down to more recent times, it appears that other experiments were made with the same object in view—viz., that of preventing the development of fungi in the tissues of the timber and planks through the fermentation of the natural juices in the wood. Sulphate of copper, sulphate of iron, creosote, and a variety of other substances were tried, but none proved so trustworthy as rock-salt.

CHAPTER V.

THE concurrent existence of two Registers was, as might have been expected, very soon found to be productive of inconvenience and other unsatisfactory consequences. At a very early period in the century the General Shipowners' Society had offered their mediation with a view to amalgamating the two Registers, but without success.

The widespread dissatisfaction, however, which had been yearly gaining strength, found expression in a succession of public meetings held by merchants and shipowners in 1823. In that year Mr. John Marshall, a shipowner of London, to whose untiring energy and sound judgment the movement owed a large measure of its success, brought the subject prominently before the annual general meeting of the Society of Shipowners, held at the London Tavern, on the 11th December, with Mr. George Lyall in the chair. Mr. Marshall has left upon record a very full account of the proceedings at this and subsequent meetings, from which we gather that by this time both the Registries of Shipping had fallen largely into disrepute, and were travelling slowly to financial ruin. A fair idea of the revenues of the Societies may be formed from the following extract from one of his speeches :—

> "The Old Book has about 180 Subscribers, at eight guineas each, and twenty guineas each from the Royal Exchange and London Assurance Companies, which gives, as I assume, an income of £1,550; the New Book has about 126 Subscribers, at the same rate, and with two similar donations, realises about £1,080. If, instead of two, only one Book was published, and that on a principle which would combine general approbation, the aggregate number of Subscribers would, I conceive, be much increased, and the ability to pay fit and competent Surveyors and other necessary and efficient officers of the establishment, proportionably augmented. The number of vessels registered in the Old Book is, in round numbers, about 14,450; in the New one, about 13,950; and upon so numerous a Marine, a revenue might, in my opinion, be raised, without any undue pressure on its Proprietors, fully adequate to the expenses of an establishment, in all respects efficient for its object."

Mr. Marshall boldly advocated radical changes in the entire organisation and administration of the Registries. He urged a change in the governing Committee, who, instead of being composed of gentlemen of one class only, "self-elected and wholly irresponsible," should consist of representatives elected by Merchants, Underwriters, and Shipowners; and he further demonstrated the necessity for a change in the system then regulating the classification of vessels, not by their intrinsic qualities, but by conditions of their age and place of build. He also disapproved of the decisions of the Surveyors being uncontrolled.

Amongst other evils of this system, complaint was made that it served to create and perpetuate an amount of tonnage for which the country was unable to find remunerative employment. Age being the great standard of classification, the effect was that, when a ship had outlived her first character, the Owner was induced immediately to sell her, from the impossibility in many trades of employing any vessel to the name of which the "talismanic charm of A 1" was not appended. The owner would then substitute a new ship, thus increasing the previously-existing glut: whereas, if classification had been based upon intrinsic merit, the owner in many cases would have effectually repaired the vessel, which would then have remained on the first class.

Upon the motion of Mr. Marshall, the meeting resolved unanimously that the present system of classing the shipping of the country was unfair in principle, injurious in its operations on the property of individuals and the efficiency and reputation of the Mercantile Marine, and misleading to those concerned with it, to the injury of all persons connected therewith, and that, with the view of effecting a revision of the system, a Committee, representative of all the interests concerned, should be appointed to obtain the fullest information on the subject, and to consider, and subsequently report, the result of their deliberations.

These resolutions received the unanimous confirmation of a large gathering of Merchants, Shipowners, and Underwriters, held under the presidency of Mr. Thomas Wilson, M.P., on the 22nd January, 1824, when the gentlemen to represent the Merchants and Shipowners on the Committee of Inquiry were elected, the Underwriters' nominees being left to the selection of the Committee of Lloyd's.

But, having arrived at this stage, the difficulties only now began. The proposal to interfere in any way with the existing systems of classification met with most determined opposition from a large and important section of the members of Lloyd's, including the Committee of that body. Mr. Benjamin Shaw, the Chairman, stated, at the meeting held at Lloyd's on the 18th February, 1824, that "although the present mode [of classing ships] might not be free from objection, yet he thought that it had been found to answer very well for the Underwriters, and therefore he should look to any alteration of the system as calling for their vigilant attention. The Committee, in the exercise of that discretion on matters affecting the interests of that House which he considered was vested in them, had given this important subject their most serious attention and consideration, since the resolutions above referred to had been officially communicated to them; and they had come to the conclusion, that the proposal of that House concurring in the proposed investigation, by appointing eight of the Members to form part of the Committee of Inquiry, was a measure which they strongly deprecated, and they had therefore prepared a written Report of their views on the subject, which he wished might be read." This document, recommending the "Subscribers to abstain from acceding to the invitation," formed the subject of an animated discussion.

Mr. Marshall made a powerful speech, traversing the Report of the Committee of Lloyd's, in the course of which he said :—

"All that is now asked for is *inquiry*; and to make that efficient, and to secure the approbation and support of all, it is proposed that all the great interests concerned shall take part in the investigation, by each appointing an equal number of persons to constitute the Committee. That this House will, on this occasion, act worthy of its character, I entertain no doubt;—celebrated, as it is, from Pole to Pole for its liberality; ever ready, as it has invariably shown itself, not only to concur, but to take the lead, in objects involving the welfare of the country, and more especially its maritime prosperity and greatness . . . Looking, sir, at the public spirit which has ever been conspicuous in the proceedings of this House—at the tone and impulse it has at different times imparted to the country, whenever its best feelings have been properly appealed to,—recollecting, too, that the very name of 'Lloyd's' is regarded, not at home only, but also in every part of the world where the British name is known, as synonymous with everything that is liberal, just, public-spirited, and honourable,—I cannot, I will not, believe, unless the conviction is forced upon me by a decision to-day contrary to my expectations, that this House will on this occasion forget, or choose to lose sight of, those great principles of equity and justice towards others by which every community must regulate its conduct, or must retrograde in its character, its considerations, and just consequence."

The result was, that the meeting resolved almost unanimously (there being but two dissentients) to nominate eight of the Members of Lloyd's to serve on the Committee of Inquiry. Still another obstacle, however, was interposed. It was found, when the day of election arrived, that most of the twenty-four gentlemen nominated on the above occasion had withdrawn their names from the ballot.

Another general meeting was accordingly called. It was held on the 3rd March, 1824. The whole subject was rediscussed at great length and with much warmth, and, the opponents of the Committee of Inquiry demanding a ballot, Wednesday, the 10th March, 1824, was fixed for that purpose, the poll "to commence at one and close at four o'clock," and to finally decide the question whether Lloyd's should or should not take part in the inquiry. Both parties exerted themselves to the utmost in the interval. The Committee of Lloyd's printed and freely circulated their Report on the subject, to which Mr. Marshall replied with a counter manifesto. Excitement ran high as the time approached for the ballot. Summing up his narrative of what occurred, Mr. Marshall says:—

> "The intense interest created by it, the feelings exhibited in its progress, and the extraordinary efforts made by most of those who so mistakenly exerted their opposition, will never be forgotten by the *friends of inquiry*, who on that day supported the moderate and reasonable proposition submitted to them. Suffice it to say, REASON TRIUMPHED! no less than *six hundred and seventy-nine Members of Lloyd's* voted on that occasion: almost every counting-house and coffee-house in the City being visited to procure the attendance of every Subscriber who could be found; the result, however, was that the Resolution 'That Lloyd's do concur in nominating eight of their Body to represent them in the Committee of Inquiry,' was confirmed on the ballot by a majority of twenty-five—there being 352 *for* and 327 *against it!*"

CHAPTER VI.

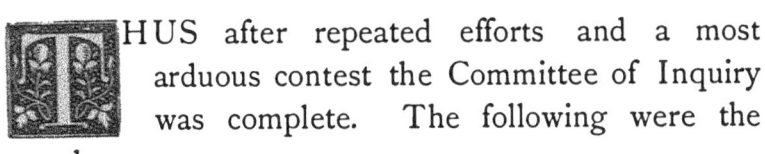

THUS after repeated efforts and a most arduous contest the Committee of Inquiry was complete. The following were the members:—

For London.

Merchants.	Shipowners.	Underwriters.
√George Palmer.	√George Lyall.	James Lindsay, jun.
William Mitchell.	George F. Young.	Arthur Willis.
Andrew Colvile.	John W. Buckle.	John Buck.
John Hodgson.	John Dawson.	Jacob Mill.
Henry Douglass.	Nath. Domett.	Robert Simpson.
John Higgin.	James Greig.	John Whitmore.
Robert Cotesworth.	Thomas Spencer.	David Carruthers.
W. M. Alexander.	Thomas Urquhart.	Thomas Ashton.

For the Outports.

Liverpool .... Edward Hurry. √?
Hull .... John Marshall.
Glasgow .... Robert Douglas.
Newcastle .... Thomas Forrest.
Whitby .... Robert Chapman.
Sunderland .... Thomas Davison.
Yarmouth .... John Diston Powles.
Leith .... David Charles Guthrie.
Whitehaven & Maryport John Simpson.

Mr. James Lindsay, jun., of Lloyd's, was appointed chairman of the Committee, whose investigation was of a most searching character, extending over a period of two years. Mr. Marshall, who it will be observed, sat on the Committee as the representative of Hull, records his conviction that "never did any Committee enter upon the duties imposed upon them with greater zeal, or a more anxious desire to acquit themselves faithfully of their obligations to the public, than the gentlemen just named; never was there exhibited a more thorough absence of every personal or private object, or a more single-hearted and earnest endeavour to render their labours practically beneficial and acceptable to *all* whose interests they were called upon, to the best of their judgment, to secure."

The Report presented by the Committee, dated the 8th February, 1826, bears ample evidence of the pains taken to obtain the fullest information. Describing the steps adopted, the Committee state that they "spared no effort to obtain from every quarter interested in the inquiry, or possessing information calculated to elucidate it, such testimony as should at once justify their recommendations and command public respect. The concurrent readiness with which their applications have been received has afforded them the advantage of obtaining the invaluable evidence and opinions of the Commissioners and Surveyors of His Majesty's Navy; of the Master-builder of His Majesty's Dockyard, Deptford; the Principal Surveyor of Shipping to the Honourable East India Company; the Surveyors to the existing Registry Books; the Shipowners' Societies at Liverpool, Hull, Sunderland, Whitehaven, and Yarmouth ; and of a considerable number of most respectable, impartial, and intelligent shipowners, brokers, agents to underwriters, shipbuilders, and others, whose long experience, high character, and extensive practical knowledge, convey abundant assurance, that, whatever may be the general opinion as to the recommendations framed on their testimony, by the Committee, the evidence itself must stand far beyond the reach of impeachment or suspicion."

The Report then proceeds to a recapitulation of the main points of the evidence brought before the Committee, from which it appears that the whole of the Merchant Shipping of the country was at that time classed in the Books printed for the avowed use of the Underwriters of Lloyd's, but supported by the general subscriptions of Merchants, Underwriters, Shipowners, and others; that the circulation of these Books was not confined to the port of London nor even to Great Britain, but was extended over every part of the Globe, and that they had become the almost universal standard by which the Merchant was guided in his shipments, the Underwriter in his insurance, and the Passenger in undertaking his voyage—in short, that the character they affixed stamped value on the ship, and almost exclusively regulated the confidence re posed in her safety and sufficiency.

Seeing that so much importance was attached to the Books, the Regulations of the governing bodies should have been on a correct basis, and the execution of these Regulations should have been entrusted to competent persons. An examination of the effect of the Books, however, showed them to be productive of many evils.

The principles adopted under the existing system of classification were "most fallacious and erroneous," while the "partial degree of actual survey required by the system" was "rendered practically nugatory by the insufficiency of the salaries paid to the Surveyors." After demonstrating the urgent necessity for terminating these "erroneous, unjust, and destructive" systems of classification, the Committee propounded a scheme for the establishment of a Registration Society on a proper basis, with a set of Rules for the Classification of Ships.

Dealing first with the Constitution of the proposed Society, the Committee observe that—"it has been their object to provide for the fair and equal representation therein of all parties immediately interested." Their proposal was as follows:—

> "That the future Superintendence of the Classification of Shipping be entrusted to a Committee in London, to be composed of thirty-two Members, consisting of six Merchants and six Shipowners of London, to be appointed by a General Meeting of Merchants and Shipowners, respectively; six Members of Lloyds, to be appointed by that body; one Representative by the Royal Exchange, London, Alliance, and Mutual Indemnity Assurance Associations, respectively; and one Representative resident in London for each of the following Outports, viz.: Liverpool, Hull, Glasgow, Newcastle, Bristol, Whitby, Yarmouth, Leith, Whitehaven, and Sunderland.
>
> "That two Members of those appointed by the Shipowners, two of those deputed by the Merchants of London, and two of the Members of Lloyd's, should go out of office annually, but be eligible for re-election; and the appointment of the Outport Representatives be during the pleasure of their Constituents.

"Such Committee to appoint a Chairman and Deputy-Chairman, Secretary, and Assistants, and all the Surveyors both for London and the Outports; and to be restricted in their proceedings to a conformity with the Rules and Regulations under which they may be appointed; but to have full power to make such Bye-Laws for their own government and proceedings as they may deem requisite, not being inconsistent with their original constitution."

In regard to Classification, the Committee, believing that the evils which they described had been "chiefly produced by the want of an enlarged and well-organised system of survey, which has been rendered impracticable by the inadequacy of the means existing for the proper remuneration of independent and competent Surveyors," proposed to establish a rigid inspection, beginning with the construction of vessels, to be carried out by a large staff of Surveyors stationed throughout the country, and subject to the supervision of Principal Surveyors appointed in London, who were to make occasional visits to the outports. Very precise instructions follow as to the conducting of the Surveyors' duties.

Vessels were to be arranged in three different classes: the First Class to comprise vessels built under survey, the number of years assigned ranging from twelve to six, according to the materials used in the construction, and also ships built in the Colonies, which were surveyed on arrival in England; the Second Class to contain ships which, being from age no longer entitled to the First Class, were still found competent to carry dry and perishable cargoes to any part of the world; the Third Class to include vessels which, although unfit for the conveyance of dry cargoes, were perfectly safe and capable of carrying cargoes not subject to sea damage.

While recommending the institution of the survey of vessels during construction, the Report does not suggest the adoption of any specific modes of construction, nor propose any scale for regulating the scantlings of new vessels, leaving full scope to the discretion of the shipbuilder and shipowner in these respects. Provision was to be made for the restoration of vessels, upon proper survey, to the first class, after the expiration of the period of years first assigned.

As regards the expenditure that would be involved in the establishment and equipment of a Register of Shipping upon the liberal basis proposed, the Committee estimated that the charges would amount in the aggregate to about £13,700 per annum, composed of £7,700 in respect of the salaries of thirty-four Surveyors,—the individual amounts ranging from £600 to £150, and, in the case of a few of the smaller ports, to £75,—and about £6,000 for the expenses of Secretary, Printing, Committee, Travelling, &c. In fixing the amount of salaries to be paid to the Surveyors, the Committee pointed out the absolute necessity of the sum being sufficient to ensure the services of men of intelligence, activity, firmness, and integrity; and added that, to the absence of regular and constant professional supervision, by properly-selected persons, the abuses and evils of the existing system had been principally traced.

Coming to deal with the important question of the

best mode of raising funds adequate to meet the expenses of the system recommended for adoption, the Committee, while preferring to leave this problem to the wisdom of the General Meeting, record their decided conviction that all expectation of raising a sum sufficient to cover the estimated expenditure "must, except under the sanction and authority of Parliamentary provision, prove visionary and hopeless." It was therefore proposed to establish the Society by means of a subsidy from the Government, the charge on the public exchequer to be met, it was suggested, by a trifling duty on tonnage or a small addition to the existing duty on Marine Insurance. The Committee at the same time admit that the "direct interposition of public support would, in all probability, transfer to the Executive Government the superintendence of a system imperatively requiring for its effective administration the aid of mercantile and professional knowledge and experience."

The fear of the Committee that a Register Society founded upon voluntary principles would not be able to raise funds equal to the establishment and maintenance of the system of classification which they sketched out, although shown by later experience to be groundless, was not so unnatural, considering the state of financial collapse into which both of the existing Registries had fallen. It is not at all unlikely that to the Committee's halting, inconclusive treatment of this question, upon which all else hinged, was largely due the fate that immediately befell their Report.

This document was presented at the general

meeting of all concerned held on the 1st June, 1826, on which occasion Mr. Thomas Wilson, M.P., was in the chair. At this meeting a letter was read from the Board of Trade, which stated, "that the Board approved highly of the proposed alterations, and were of opinion that it would give rise to great improvement in the naval architecture of the country; and that the Lords of their Committee would be disposed to assist in carrying the proposed regulations into effect, in any manner which might, on subsequent discussion, be deemed advisable." Beyond this offer, the Board declined to make any positive announcement which might be held to commit the Government.

A subsequent meeting was appointed to be held to discuss the proposals. The consideration of the subject, however, was from one cause and another adjourned from time to time without any decision being arrived at; until, in consequence, as would appear, of the sudden death of two of the principal leaders of the movement, and of the opposition offered to the scheme from some quarters, and the indifference manifested in others, the supporters of the proposed system were induced to desist from pursuing it farther at that time.

CHAPTER VII.

SEVERAL years elapsed before any effectual steps were taken in furtherance of the Object, but the gradual decay of the two Registries greatly strengthened the position of those who advocated the entire reorganisation of the existing systems of classification.

The Shipowners' Book had, it is stated, been carried on at an annual loss, and the effect of the competition appears to have told upon the finances of its older rival, as will be seen from a statement published with the Green Book for 1828-29, which runs as follows:—

"LLOYD'S REGISTRY OF SHIPPING,
"CASTLE COURT, BIRCHIN LANE,
"*January*, 1829.

"The Committee beg leave to remind the Subscribers that when this Society was established, in the year 1760, the Annual Subscription was Twelve Guineas.

"At the end of Half a Century, their funded Property having increased to £12,000 Stock, the Price of the Book was reduced one-third, viz., from Twelve to

Eight Guineas; but the Expenses for the last Twenty Years having exceeded the Income by nearly £500 per Annum, and the Stock now remaining amounting to only £2,000, the Committee are under the necessity of raising the Price of the Book this Year to Ten Guineas.

"Nearly Ten Thousand Vessels are surveyed every Year; the Expense of Survey, by competent Judges, cannot be reduced under the present Salaries, which exceed £1,000 per annum, rather under 2s. 1½d. each vessel."

The impossibility of reducing the salaries of the Surveyors will not be disputed when it is mentioned that the two principal Surveyors in London were receiving only £250 per annum *between them* at this period!

It is worthy of notice that in this announcement we find the first assumption of the name of "Lloyd's," as prefixed to a Register of Shipping—preceding books having been styled "Registers" only.

In 1833 we find both of the Registries in so desperate a state that it was not expected they would be able to carry on their operations beyond another year or two. The "Special Committee on the affairs of Lloyd's," fearing that under these circumstances the community might be left without a Book, and with the object of rendering the inspection of shipping more efficient, appointed a Sub-Committee to confer with the Committees of the two bodies, and endeavour to effect a union between them. On the 14th August, 1833, a meeting was held in the Merchant Seamen's Office, of which the following copy of a minute, signed by the members of the "Special Committee," now exists :—

"The Sub-Committee to whom it was referred at the last meeting to confer with the Committees of the two Register Books beg to report that they met for that purpose, in this office, on Tuesday, the 13th inst., the following gentlemen on behalf of the Red Book, viz.:—

    Mr. Lancaster,   Mr. Hall,
    Mr. Palmer,   Mr. Harrison,
        Mr. Willis;

And the following on behalf of the Green Book, viz.:—

    Mr. Harford,   Mr. Luke,
    Mr. Kerr,   Mr. Carruthers,
    Mr. Dawson,   Mr. W. G. Shedden.

And that, after much discussion, the following resolutions were carried unanimously, with an understanding that, if any obstacle should arise on the part of the Shipowners' Society to carrying the same into effect, an early communication thereof should be made to this Committee by the Committee of the Red Book.

"1st. That it is not practicable to carry on the two Register Books as at present circumstanced.

"2nd. That in the opinion of this meeting it is desirable that an union of the Committees of the two Registers take place for the purpose of establishing one good and efficient Register.—

    "(Signed) R. DEWAR,
          J. MILL,
          S. SMITH,
          J. SIMPSON,
          W. F. SADLER."

Mr. Sadler, writing at the same date to Mr. Lancaster, Chairman of the Red Book, on behalf of the Special Committee on the affairs of Lloyd's, expressed their earnest hope that he would, in conjunction with the Committee of the other Book, take early measures for carrying into effect a resolution which appeared to the Special Committee to be of vital importance to the shipping and commercial interests of the country.

No opposition being offered by the General Shipowners' Society to the proposed fusion of the existing Books, a meeting of the Committees of the two Registries was held on Thursday, the 10th October, 1833, at the River Dee office, over the Royal Exchange, at which the under-mentioned gentlemen were present:—

George Palmer, Charles Harford,
Nathaniel Domett, David Carruthers,
J. W. Buckle, Thomas Chapman,
George Allfrey, Joseph Somes,
John Luke, J. Dawson,
W. N. Lancaster, Crawford D. Kerr,
Thomas Hall, Henry Cheape.

Mr. Palmer was appointed Chairman, while Mr. Chapman consented to act as Honorary Secretary, discharging the duties of this office during the period covered by the first six meetings of the Committee.

It was then resolved to form the Members of the two Committees into a Joint Committee for carrying the proposed union into effect, the principal details of the scheme being remitted to the consideration of a Sub-Committee. The first outline of a Constitution is contained in the Minutes of the second meeting of the United Committee on the 24th October, at which the following resolutions were passed:—

"That a Society be established for obtaining an accurate classification of the Mercantile Marine of the United Kingdom, and of the Foreign vessels trading thereto, and that a Book be annually printed, to be called 'The Register Book of British and Foreign Shipping.'

"That all persons subscribing the sum of Three Guineas annually be Members of the Society, and entitled (for their own use) to a copy of the Register Book.

"That the affairs of the Society be conducted by a Committee of twenty-one Members, who shall elect from amongst themselves a Chairman and Deputy-Chairman, and be empowered to fill up vacancies, and that five be the quorum.

"That such of the present Members of the Two Committees as shall signify their assent thereto, shall be Members of the New Committee."

Further regulations were also adopted respecting the subscriptions of Marine Insurance Companies and public establishments, the appointment of Surveyors, and the scale of Fees to be charged. Respecting the classification of vessels, it was decided to adopt, with some alterations, the Rules for Classification laid down in the printed Report of the Committee of 1824, the first "Instructions to Surveyors" drawn up being also founded upon the recommendations of that document. These Rules formed the subject of a conference between Sub-Committees of the projected Society and of the General Shipowners' Society, comprising the following gentlemen :—

Representing the Registry Committee.

Arthur Willis,	B. McGhie,
Charles Harford,	John Luke,
Henry Nelson,	Thomas Chapman,
Nathaniel Domett,	George Allfrey,

Joseph Somes.

Representing the General Shipowners' Society.

George F. Young,	Robert Barry,
Octavius Wigram,	Robert Carter,
William Tindall,	Henry Buckle.

The Rules then underwent very material alterations, and in their amended form were adopted at a meeting of the United Committee of the Registry on the 17th January, 1834, and ordered to be published in the form of a " Prospectus of the Plan for the Establishment of a New Register Book of British and Foreign Shipping." From this document it appears that the existing Committee were to be considered merely as a Provisional Committee for arranging and completing the establishment of the Society on the following basis :—

All persons subscribing the sum of three guineas annually were to be Members of the Society, and entitled, *for their own use*, to a copy of the Register Book; the subscription of Public Establishments being fixed at ten guineas, with the exception of that of the four Marine Insurance Companies in London, namely, the Royal Exchange, London, Alliance, and Mutual Indemnity, which had each agreed to give an annual subscription of one hundred guineas.

The superintendence of the affairs of the Society was to be entrusted to a Committee in London, to be composed of twenty-four Members, consisting of an equal proportion of *Merchants, Shipowners, and Underwriters*, and in addition the Chairman of Lloyd's and the Chairman of the General Shipowners' Society, for the time, were to be *ex-officio* Members of the Committee.

The Provisional Committee were in the first instance to appoint the eight Members constituting the mercantile portion of the Permanent Committee; the Committee of the General Shipowners' Society to elect the eight Members constituting the portion of Shipowners; and the Committee of Lloyd's the eight Members to represent the Underwriters.

The vacancies thereafter arising through the annual retirement, by rotation, of six of the Members, namely, two of each of the constituent parts of the Committee (who would be eligible for re-election), were to be filled up by the election of two Shipowners and one Merchant by the Committee of the General Shipowners' Society, and two Underwriters and one Merchant by the Committee of Lloyd's.

The Committee were to have full power to make such Bye-Laws for their own government and proceedings as they might deem requisite, not being inconsistent with the original Rules and Regulations under which the Society was established.

After stating the conditions attaching to the appointment of Surveyors to the Society, the Prospectus proceeds to explain the general principles which the Committee had determined to adopt for their guidance in the future classification of ships, and which are sufficiently clear from the first resolution under this head, namely:—

> "That the characters to be assigned shall be, as nearly as circumstances will permit, a correct indication of the real and intrinsic quality of the ship; and that the same shall no longer be regulated, as heretofore, by the incorrect standard of the port of building, nor on the decision of the Surveyors; but will henceforward be in all cases finally affixed by the Committee, after a due inspection of the Reports of the Surveyors and the documents which may be submitted to them."

In regard to the funds of the Society, which it was

provided should be under the authority and control of the Committee, it was decided that the revenue should not depend solely upon the subscriptions to the Register Book, as had evidently been the case with the preceding Register Societies. The subscription to the Register Book, it will be observed, was fixed at a very low figure, but, in addition, fees were to be charged to shipowners for the survey and classification of vessels according to an approved scale.

It is evident, from the records of the Provisional Committee, that they at one time contemplated the necessity of receiving some pecuniary assistance from the Government in furtherance of the objects of the Society. Mr. George Lyall, M.P., a member of the Committee, was deputed to seek an interview with the President and Vice-President of the Board of Trade, and to enter fully into an explanation of the intended proceedings of the Society, and urge the claims of the Society to national support. When it appeared from this gentleman's inquiries on the subject that no expectation of pecuniary assistance from the public funds could be relied upon, it became a serious question with the Committee whether sufficient confidence could be placed in their prospects to enable the Society to proceed with the means that might now be calculated upon.

A Sub-Committee of Finance was specially appointed to investigate the expected resources upon which dependence might be placed for proceeding with the proposed undertaking; and their report, which contains an elaborate estimate based upon the experience of the two preceding Registers and the total tonnage of the country, concluded with the opinion that the Committee were justified, under all the circumstances, in proceeding with the scheme.

An application to the Government to obtain the privilege of transmitting reports of surveys from the outport Surveyors free of charge in those days of heavy postage proved equally unavailing. The Committee's appeal to Shipowners and Underwriters, however, for contributions to the Society, with the view of expediting the appointment of Surveyors and the arrangements necessary for the issue of the new Book, was productive of better results. The Subscribers to Lloyd's, at a general meeting, upon the motion of Mr. Arthur Willis, a member of that body and also of the Provisional Committee, unanimously voted a sum of £1,000 from their funds in aid of the Society, and individual Underwriters contributed over £700; while, in addition to the annual subscription of 100 guineas which the London Assurance Corporation and the Alliance Marine Assurance Company had agreed upon, they each gave a donation of 50 guineas, and the West India Dock Company one of 30 guineas. It should be mentioned that the amount received from Lloyd's was repaid to that Institution a few years afterwards, when the funds of the Society permitted.

The Provisional Committee continued to manage the affairs of the Society until October, 1834—framing the Rules for Classification, selecting and appointing Surveyors and other officers, examining the reports of survey sent in by the Surveyors, classifying the ships for entry in the Register Book, and making all necessary arrangements for the preparation and issue of the Book. At first the Committee met two or three times a week, but the pressure of business had become so great by June, 1834, that on the 27th of that month it was decided that the General Committee should " be convened to meet on Tuesday next, the 1st July, at eleven o'clock, and that from and after that day the Committee will *sit daily*" for the transaction of business. Having brought their labours to a satisfactory termination by the production of the first edition of " LLOYD'S REGISTER OF BRITISH AND FOREIGN SHIPPING," they dissolved on the 21st of October, 1834, and handed over their trust to the Permanent Committee, which had by that time been appointed.

CHAPTER VIII.

THE Permanent Committee was composed of the under-mentioned gentlemen:—

MERCHANTS
(Appointed by the Provisional Committee).

T. W. Buckle.
T. A. Curtis.
Thomson Hankey, jun.
George Hanson.
Crawford D. Kerr.
George Lyall, M.P.
Alexander Mitchell.
Patrick M. Stewart, M.P.

SHIPOWNERS
(Elected by the Committee of the General Shipowners' Society).

Thomas Benson.
Nathaniel Domett.
Richard Drew.
B. A. McGhie.
Joseph Somes.
William Tindall.
Thomas Ward.
George F. Young, M.P.

UNDERWRITERS
(Elected by the Committee of Lloyd's).

George Allfrey.
David Carruthers.
Thomas Chapman.
Henry Cheape.
William Marshall.
John Robinson.
R. H. Shepard.
Arthur Willis.

Chairman of Lloyd's.
George R. Robinson, M.P.

Chairman of the General Shipowners' Society.
Octavius Wigram.

Mr. David Carruthers was elected Chairman of the Permanent Committee, and Mr. Crawford D. Kerr the Deputy-Chairman. For a period of about two months, in 1833, Mr. Chapman had served as the Honorary Secretary to the Provisional Committee, and, as will be seen, his name appears in the list of the Permanent Committee of 1834-35. But upon Mr. Kerr's retirement, through ill-health, Mr. Chapman was elected on the 9th April, 1835, to the office of Deputy-Chairman, and on the 25th June of the same year, shortly after the death of Mr. Carruthers, he was appointed Chairman of the Society.

Mr. Nathaniel Symonds, who acted as Secretary to the Committee until January, 1837, was then succeeded by Mr. Charles Graham, who had previously been in the service of the Lords Commissioners of the Admiralty.

We have now reached the period when the present Register Book came into existence, and it will be of interest to pause here and consider the circumstances of the British Mercantile Marine at this time, especially in their relation to the Society's earliest operations. In 1834 a vessel of 500 tons was considered large, and the tonnage built in each of the several preceding years bears but a very small proportion to that of to-day. For instance, there were built—

Year.	In the United Kingdom.	In British Colonies.
In 1830	750 vessels.	367 vessels.
,, 1831	760 ,,	376 ,,
,, 1832	759 ,,	221 ,,

Of the 750 vessels built in 1830, the tonnage was composed as follows :—

About 210 were under 50 tons.
„ 200 „ 100 „
„ 150 „ 200 „
„ 150 „ 300 „
„ 30 „ 400 „
and 10 above 500 „

The large proportion of vessels built in the Colonies—chiefly North American—is also an item worthy of attention in examining these statistics.

Of the vessels belonging to the United Kingdom in 1830 the following is a summary of the tonnages :—

50 tons and under	6,542 ships.
50 tons to 100	5,212 „
100 „ 200	3,942 „
200 „ 300	1,948 „
300 „ 400	969
400 „ 500	329
500 „ 800	110
800 „ 1,000	15
1,200 and upwards	43
Total	19,110 „

In addition to these there were 4,547 vessels of 330,227 tons registered in the British Colonies.

In 1833 we find that the Underwriters' Register, or Green Book, contained 16,615 ships, and that the number recorded in the rival Shipowners' Register, or Red Book, was 15,670.

It need hardly be said that all this tonnage was of wood, as no iron ship appears in the Register Book until the year 1837.

The Register Book as issued in 1834—a reprint of a page of which appears on the opposite side—contained a record of all vessels of 50 tons and upwards registered in the United Kingdom, whether classed or not, and the following particulars, as far as they could be ascertained, were given:—The name and description of the vessel, the name of the master, the tonnage, the port and year of build, the name of the owner, the port of registry, and the classification, if assigned, together with the port at which the vessel had been surveyed. There were also abbreviated descriptions of the material of which the vessel was built, and of the repairs executed.

The form and arrangement of the Book, as determined in 1834, remained practically unaltered for many years. The first volume necessarily contained but a small proportion of classed to unclassed vessels, as characters were assigned only after survey by the Society's Officers. In this respect, and also as regards the amount of the information it contained, the new Register Book would not bear comparison with the issue of either of its predecessors; and there appear to have been many complaints of vessels being entered in it without a class. The reason for including ships not classed is obvious. It was impossible, under the rules adopted by the Committee, to assign a character to the vessels already afloat until they had been surveyed and reported upon by the Society's Surveyors. If the volume had contained only the particulars of the vessels which had been classed by the Committee up to the time of its issue, it

Ships.	Masters.	Tons	BUILD. Where.	BUILD. When.	Owners.	Port belonging to.	Destined Voyage.	No.Years first assigned	Character for Hulls Stores. Classification
n Hill Sr pts.&C.29	Richards	163	Qubec O.&E	1828	R Thomas	Watrfrd	Liv. Hmbro		Æ 1 2
Alexander mmond	T.Cuthill	282				London			
—M'Ken- Bg	Williams	124	Strnwy ND.W.& T Sds	1818 30	W. Coffin	Cardiff	Cff. Watrfrd		Æ 1 7
oucher W Sr	J. Ray T. Wadley	88	Ilfracb RB.O.&F;	1828	Swainst	Ilfr'cmb Liverpool	Liv. Coastr	7	A 1 10
harles For S C.32	J. Leslie	364	Abrdn	1824	Boothby	London Liverpool	Fal.		Æ 1 10
M'Car- F.&C 34	J. Walker	188	Bklrsd trp.34	1821	J. Walker	London	Lon.C.G.H. Restored 1834	5 Yrs	A 1 8
		3	O.B.B.E.&F ND.29 I.of Wt	1827	M'Neice	London	Lon.C.G.H.	10	A 1 7
		0				London			
dward Ba	Bennett	72				London			
	A. Bruce	105				Aberd'n			
	Norwood	180				London			
Hamil- S F.&s.3	R. Lundy	483	Lond trp.32	1836	T. Ward	Brdlgtn	Hal. Amer		E 1 9
	Newbolt	471				London			
Paget	R. Martin	482				London			
incis Bur S F.&C.32	W Dunbar F.Scott	411	Quebc	1825	D. Gibb	Liverp'l	Liv. Africa		1 2
Drake Sr	G.Nichols	113	Plymh trp.33	1823	Capt.& C	Plym'th	Fal. Prtsmh		E 1 12
Yessel C.26,pt33	M.C.								
eorge Mu Bk F.&s.32	J. Beverly	327	P.E.Isl B.B.& Y.P.	1829	W. Lens	Liverp'l	Liv. Bathrst		E 7
enry Stan e	J.Johnson	85				London			
umphrey	J. Brown	65				Nwcastl			
nes Cock	G. Allen	366				London			
Kempt C.32	J. Patrick	304	N.Scb B.B.Hks P.	1826 trp.32	J. Wait	Dundee	Dun. Baltic		Æ 1 9
inBerres	J. Collin	292				Liverp'l			
Byng Bg C.32	W. Cram	141	Poole	1832	Fryer&Co	Poole	Poo.Nwfl'nd	10	A 1 8
Franklin w C.	Mitch'nsn J.Corner	244	Sthwk	1833	Barton &c	Nwcastl Liverpl	Liv. Mntral	U	A 1 4

face p. 56.

would have been of but small dimensions, and of little service to the public. The succeeding editions of the work, however, bear testimony to the extensive scale of the Society's operations. During the first five years of its existence no fewer than 15,000 surveys of vessels had been held, and the reports thereof dealt with by the Committee. The decision, therefore, to omit, upon reprinting the book in 1838, vessels which had never been surveyed and classed, made no appreciable difference in the bulk of the volume.

The Rules and Regulations as finally adopted by the Provisional Committee, and in the framing of which Mr. G. F. Young, M.P., and Mr. William Tindall took a leading part, treated of the construction of wood ships in brief and general terms, and contained but slight reference to the building of wood steamers, which until that time had been comparatively few in number. There was little direction laid down beyond the description of timber to be used in the construction of vessels for the respective terms of classification, and the scantlings of the principal parts of a vessel. Four different grades of classification were provided, based substantially upon the Rules drawn up by the Mixed Committee of Inquiry in 1826, the methods of distinguishing the classes previously in vogue being followed by the new Society.

The letter A indicated the first description of the First Class, which included ships that had not passed a prescribed age, and were kept in the highest state of efficiency.

The character Æ denoted the second description

of the First Class, and applied to vessels which had passed the prescribed age, and had not undergone the repairs required for Continuation or Restoration on the A character, but were still in a condition for the safe conveyance of dry and perishable cargoes.

The letter E designated the Second Class, comprising ships which, although unfit for carrying dry cargoes, were perfectly safe for the conveyance, to all parts of the world, of cargoes not in their nature liable to sea damage.

The Third Class, denoted by the letter I, included vessels which were good in constitution and fit for the conveyance on short voyages (not out of Europe) of cargoes not subject to sea damage.

The condition of the anchors, cables, and stores, when satisfactory, was indicated by the figure 1; when unsatisfactory, by the figure 2.

New ships, to be entitled to rank in the first description of the first class, for the full period provided by the Rules, must have been inspected, while building, by the Society's Surveyors. The prescribed examination was very like that now prescribed for vessels building under "ordinary survey"; which is to say that they were examined at certain stages of their construction, and not continuously, as is required in the present day for vessels building under "special survey."

As regards vessels already in existence at the establishment of the new Register, and which, as intimated, were required to undergo a careful survey at the hands of the Society's officers prior to classification, it was stated that "they would be classed agreeably to the descriptions laid down for the building of new ships, unless on such survey there were found sufficient cause to assign them a less period."

But while a sufficiently favourable opportunity was thus afforded to owners of existing ships to secure a class equal to that which would have been granted if the vessels had been built under survey, the same latitude was not extended to those built subsequently to the promulgation of the Rules. In the case of such vessels, one year was to be deducted from the class which would otherwise have been awarded; and in 1842 this regulation was so altered that a vessel not built under survey could be classed no higher than 10 A.

So early as 1834 the importance of keeping wood vessels dry during construction was understood, and an extra year was added to the period for which they might be classed, provided they were built under an efficient roof, and twelve months were occupied in their construction.

After the expiration of the term of years originally assigned to vessels on the A character, they could be restored to that grade, under certain restrictions, at any age, if found upon surveys of a most searching character to be in a satisfactory condition. Indeed, the requirements of the Rules in this respect were far in excess of any now in operation, and it is perhaps somewhat surprising that this severity does not appear to have raised complaints from any quarter at the time. The Rules on this point were, however, in accordance with the best practice of the period, as exemplified by the ordinary routine of the East India Company in the periodical examination of their vessels.

If a vessel was not restored to the A class, she lapsed into the second description of the first class, designated Æ, provided her condition was sufficiently good; it being considered that vessels of this description were fit to carry dry and perishable cargoes. Restored vessels also lapsed into the Æ class upon the same conditions.

The Rules issued in 1834 contained precise regulations regarding the survey of steamers, the number of such vessels having been gradually increasing for several years prior to that date. It was provided that they should be surveyed twice in each year; and that at the above directed surveys a certificate from some competent Master Engineer should be produced, a notation to this effect being made in the Register Book.

It is worthy of note that, under the provisions of the Rules in force at this time, and for about twenty years later, the scantlings allowed for wood steamers under 300 tons were required to be only equal to two-thirds of those prescribed for sailing ships of the same tonnage, the proportion being altered to three-fourths in steamers of larger size.

To conduct the surveys prescribed by the Rules of the new Committee, a staff of Surveyors was appointed, numbering sixty-three in all, of whom thirteen were exclusively the servants of the Society, and these were distributed at the different ports in the United Kingdom, in proportion to the average amount of tonnage built at or sailing from the district. The exclusive Surveyors were appointed thus:—

District.	Number of Surveyors.
Bristol	1
Glasgow, Greenock, and ports on the Clyde	1
Hull, Gainsborough, Goole, Selby, Thorn, and Grimsby	2
Leith and ports in the Frith of Forth	1
Liverpool	2
London	3
Newcastle and Shields	1
Sunderland	2
Total	13

These Surveyors were of two classes, known as "Shipwright Surveyors" and "Nautical Surveyors." The former were practical shipwrights, who had served an apprenticeship in the usual manner; whereas the latter were shipmasters possessing an acquaintance with the construction and repairs of ships. The primary duty of the Nautical Surveyors appears to have been to attend to the survey of vessels afloat, and that of the Shipwright Surveyors the inspection of vessels while building, while both officers joined in the surveys on old vessels in dry dock; but this division of labour could only be adopted in the principal ports which had surveyors of both classes.

The duty of classifying ships upon the Surveyors' reports was at first undertaken by the whole Committee; but in 1835 it was delegated to Sub-Committees.

The earliest list of these Sub-Committees is dated April 9th, 1835.

The changes made in the Rules of the Society during the earlier years of its existence were not very considerable. In 1837, a new class, *Æ in *red*, was introduced, to represent vessels of a superior character to those previously given the Æ class, the red colour having been probably chosen to distinguish the vessels readily from others classed with the same letter in the Book. Ships so classed were fit to carry dry and perishable cargoes to and from all parts of the world, and had lapsed from the A class without having completed such repairs as were necessary for restoration or continuation to the first class.

In the year 1837 the Rule for the continuation of ships on the highest class was first given. This continuation was not to exceed one-third the number of years originally assigned, and was to begin from the expiration of the original class, and not from the date of survey. The opening out of the vessel was, it seems, left to the judgment of the Surveyor, and not carefully prescribed as at present. This was the only Rule in operation under which a vessel was eligible for continuation on the A 1 character until 1863, when, by a more stringent examination of the vessel's frame, an extension of two-thirds the original class was granted. These two terms of continuation—viz., the one-third and the two-third terms—were supplemented, in 1881, by a third Rule, which provided that the vessel might be again continued at the end of the ordinary continuation period, such continuation not to exceed one-third the number of years originally assigned.

In 1837, carefully-prepared Tables were first introduced into the Rules, specifying the different periods of classification which would be assigned by the Committee to vessels built of certain different kinds of wood, and stating the several parts of the vessel in which these woods might be used for the respective terms of years.

CHAPTER IX.

THE new Society was now, in 1834, an aecomplished fact, and although, perhaps, it did not fully realise in all respects the perfect ideal of a National Registry of Shipping, it was unquestionably an immense improvement upon the previously existing Registries. Now, for the first time, the classification of the Mercantile Marine was entrusted to a large Committee directly representative, not of one section only, but of the whole of the interests concerned, namely, the Merchant, the Underwriter, and Shipowner; and now also, for the first time, was there a serious and systematic attempt made to put into actual practice the principle of assigning the character of a vessel according to her intrinsic merits.

Coming after the promulgation of a scheme of representation drawn on such broad and liberal lines as those laid down in the Report of the Committee of Inquiry in 1826, it was, perhaps, scarcely to be expected that the constitution of the Committee of Management of the new Registry, although infinitely superior to that of the Boards of its predecessors, should command universal approval. The members of the Committee, it was true, were elected by each of the several interests involved, but they were drawn from the shipping community of London alone, the outports having no direct voice in the choice of representatives. The Committee who framed the constitution of the Society expressed their " earnest desire to cultivate and maintain the most perfect good understanding with the Merchants, Shipowners, and Underwriters of the different ports of the United Kingdom, on whose support and co-operation they rely for the promotion of the objects of the Institution within their respective districts," and they sought, and in many cases obtained, the advice and assistance of commercial bodies at the different ports in the selection of properly qualified Surveyors.

The desire of the principal outports, however, to possess a more direct representation in the management of the Society was evinced at a very early period. Soon after the publication of the Prospectus in the beginning of 1834, the Committee were called upon to consider the question. The first communication on the subject was received from Sunderland,— then the most important shipbuilding centre in the country, nearly equalling, as regards the number and tonnage of ships built, all the other ports together. This was quickly followed by a representation from Liverpool, then, as now, the great centre of the West, in all matters pertaining to merchant shipping. The objections emanating from the latter port were at first confined to the proposed scale of charges The establishment of a local Committee affiliated to the Committee of the Society was next suggested. It appears, however, that the powers desired for the proposed Liverpool Committee were greater than could be granted consistently with the constitution of the Society, and therefore negotiations were ultimately abandoned.

The Liverpool people upon the rejection of their proposals endeavoured to establish another Register of Shipping, and there was issued in the following year (1835) a book bearing the title of the "Liverpool Register of Shipping," containing the names and other particulars, but not the characters, of vessels belonging to Liverpool and of those trading thereto. There appears to have been but this one issue of the work.

During the next few years the constitution of the Society and its practical working were freely canvassed in the mercantile press. In the course of time the opposition of parties at the outports was, for the most part, conciliated by the action of the General Shipowners' Society. To this body was entrusted the election of one-half of the members of the Register Committee, and when filling up vacancies care was taken to include a fair proportion of such members of the Shipowners' Society as held seats there as the representatives of outports. By this means we find that in one year, out of the twelve gentlemen returned by the Shipowners' Society to serve on the Committee of Lloyd's Register, no less than five were the nominees of outports, namely of Whitby, Sunderland, Scarborough, South Shields, and North Shields.

In Liverpool, however, this arrangement was not considered quite satisfactory, and a guarantee fund was raised in April, 1838, for the creation of a separate Register. The outcome of this movement was the "Liverpool Register of Shipping," which appears to have closely imitated Lloyd's Register, both in the symbols of classification and in the arrangement and phraseology of the Rules.

In 1844, a proposal was made by the Committee of the Liverpool Book that the two Societies should make a common revision of their respective Rules, in order to remove the differences that existed between them, and so put an end to any attempt to play off one Society against the other. Upon the invitation of the Committee of Lloyd's Register, the Liverpool Committee forwarded their suggestions on the Rules, and concluded by stating that, should their views be adopted, one Book would be sufficient.

The propositions put forward by the Liverpool Committee involved the existence of two Boards of Management, having equal powers within their respective provinces,—one at Liverpool having sole control of that district, and the other in London having jurisdiction over the other ports of the country. To this the General Committee could not consent, as it would have been inconsistent with the "fundamental constitution of this Society," but they referred the proposed amendments of the Rules to the consideration of a Sub-Committee. Negotiations now closed, but were reopened next year. A common ground of agreement was discovered, and on the 28th April, 1845, the amalgamation of the two bodies was finally approved of by the General Committee in special meeting assembled.

The basis of amalgamation was substantially as follows:—The Liverpool Branch Committee, it was arranged, should consist of twelve Members, who would be elected by the Liverpool Underwriters Association and Shipowners' Association in equal proportions, the Chairmen of the Associations of Shipowners, Underwriters, and Shipbuilders respectively remaining *ex-officio* Members. The Chairman and Deputy-Chairman of the local Committee, together with the Chairman of the local Classification Committee, were each to have a seat at the London Board, *ex officio*. In dealing with reports of surveys held in the Liverpool district, the Branch Committee would stand in much the same relation as the Sub-Committee of Classification in London to the General Committee, whose decision on all reports of survey, as well as on other matters, is final.

It was further distinctly specified that none of these arrangements should restrict the London Committee from the exercise of a general superintendence over the affairs of the Society, in the Liverpool district, as elsewhere, as prescribed by the Rules. Such vessels as were classed exclusively in the Liverpool Register Book were to be placed in an appendix to Lloyd's Register, to be discontinued after a few years, the difference in the Rules of the two Societies being made the subject of consideration.

CHAPTER X.

WHILE these constitutional questions were being discussed and arranged, there were also heard sounds of murmuring against the proceedings of the still young Register Society in another respect. Prior to the publication of the Rules for the classification of vessels, the principles of theoretical naval architecture were little known. The country doubtless, had many very good shipbuilders, who built good and efficient vessels, but they were seldom guided by scientific rules. No scale of scantlings for the principal parts of merchant ships had been in force, nor was the practice of the preceding Register Societies, as regards new ships, based upon reliable data; while, alike as regards the construction of new vessels and the efficient repairing of old ones, there was entirely wanting any well-arranged or uniform system of inspection. The Surveyors under the old arrangement, as has already been pointed out, were left practically uncontrolled in their decisions, and assigned characters in the Register Books to the vessels which they themselves surveyed.

But now there was introduced by the Society's Rules a uniformity of system based upon the best ascertained practice, which left no room for glaring differences between the practice of one locality and another and the judgment of different Surveyors. The presiding Committee now granted classes to vessels only upon evidence of the requirements of the Rules having been complied with.

The transition from the old, loose practice to the new systematic course of procedure was naturally attended with no small difficulties. Shipowners and shipbuilders, who had hitherto been left to follow their own inclinations in many cases, did not take kindly to the altered circumstances, and, as a result, the Society gained a notoriety in some quarters for being arbitrary and too strict in its requirements.

Added to all this, the commercial marine of the country was then passing through a period of severe depression, which was not calculated to awaken shipowners to a lively interest in a Register Society that, constituted as it was, must depend entirely for support upon them and the other interests concerned.

Under these circumstances, it is not surprising to learn that for the first two or three years of the Society's existence it was somewhat doubtful whether it would succeed. The Subscribers to the Register Book, who on the establishment of the Society in 1834 numbered 721, had dwindled down in two years to 615; and in 1836, when Christmas came round, the funds were at such a low ebb that Mr. Chapman, the Chairman, advanced a sum of money in order that the salaries of the officers might not be in arrear! This, however, was the turning-point, the "darkest hour before the dawn"; for prosperity soon afterwards attended the Committee's efforts, and there was never a recurrence of this state of things. The Rules of the Society by this time had gained a hold on the public, and the number of Subscribers to the work rapidly increased from year to year, until the Committee had the satisfaction and pride of seeing the Institution which they had brought into existence take up a position of the first importance in the confidence of the public,—one that the vicissitudes of fifty years have left unimpaired.

A brief reference to some of the contemporary records containing evidence of the estimation in which the Society was then held, may not be without interest. The Report of the Select Committee of the House of Commons, appointed in the year 1836, to inquire into the causes of the increased number of shipwrecks, furnishes us with the opinions of shipowners and others who gave evidence, and with the judgment of the Select Committee itself, in regard to the operations and influence of the Register.

It seems that at that time there was a feeling of uneasiness in some quarters regarding the apparent increase in the number of shipwrecks, and in connexion with a question of such importance affecting the mercantile marine it could only be expected that the Society's work would come under consideration. The Select Committee in their Report explain the shortcomings of the old Register Societies, to whose defective systems of classification they show that the production of cheap and badly-constructed ships was chiefly due; and they then go on to say that "the system of classification has been greatly improved by the formation of a new Association, entitled, 'Lloyd's Register of British and Foreign Shipping,' the basis of whose regulations appears to be a *bonâ-fide* attempt to classify vessels according to their real and intrinsic merits, including their age, construction, materials, workmanship, and stores"; also that "there is reason to believe that the ultimate result of this new system of classification will be to effect a great improvement in the general character of the ships of the United Kingdom." That this expectation has since been realised is doubtless the opinion of all who have carefully watched the successive developments in naval construction during later years, and have traced the effects of the Society's influence in relation to them.

The Annual Report presented to the public meeting of the General Shipowners' Society in July, 1840, bears testimony to the continued growth of the Society, which is alluded to in the following terms:—

"The last point to which your Committee would especially call attention is one which involves probably a greater degree of real importance than any other charge entrusted to their superintendence. It is the position occupied by the Committee in relation to the now really national establishment of 'Lloyd's Register of British and Foreign Shipping.' The vast influence over the Shipping property of the country exercised by that Committee, though by some imperfectly understood, and by many inadequately estimated, may be inferred from the fact that 11,595 ships and vessels are now recorded in the Register." * * *

"It is the unhesitating belief of your Committee that,

making reasonable allowance for difficulties inseparable from such a task, this important duty is, on the whole, ably, impartially, and beneficially performed; the general character of British Shipping having considerably improved since the establishment of the new system."

The views of the Committee received confirmation from the speeches delivered at the meeting, one outport representative stating that, to his knowledge, the "improvement in shipbuilding at Sunderland was greatly due to the action of Lloyd's Register."

Some interesting evidence to the same effect is found in the proceedings of the Select Committee of the House of Commons of 1843 on "Shipwrecks." The Committee's report contains the following paragraph:—

> "The Association formed for the survey and classification of merchant vessels, especially alluded to in the report of the Committee of 1836, under the name of 'Lloyd's Register of British and Foreign Shipping,' has made regular progress from that time, and, as appears by the evidence of the Secretary, any objections entertained against it in the first instance are now removed, and shipowners are generally ready to submit their ships and stores to the fair examination of the surveyors of the Society for the purpose of having them classed in the Register Book according to their real quality."

By this time Shippers and Passengers, as well as Underwriters, were in the habit of consulting the Register Book before they embarked their goods, their persons, or their money upon a ship to risk the hazards of a voyage, believing that when information respecting a ship was not to be obtained by reference to the Register it was a "bad omen and a weighty objection against her." We now find the *Shipping and Mercantile Gazette*, which, in the earlier existence of the Society, had been one of its most candid critics, constrained to admit that the Committee of the new Society had "exercised their functions with honour, firmness, and impartiality"; and that the system of classification "brought into operation under all the difficulties of a declining trade, had attained a success which, considering the want of unanimity among Shipowners, is very remarkable." Again, the same journal stated that the Registry had by this time "acquired so great an importance as an authority upon the value and seaworthiness of merchant vessels, that it would be impossible for ever so good a ship to obtain freight abroad without reference to the Register."

The following figures show the progress made in the classification of ships between 1836 and 1842:—

Number of vessels classed A in	1836	...	2,789
„	„	„	1837	...	3,186
			1838	...	3,782
			1839	...	4,401
			1840	...	5,226
			1841	...	5,961
			1842	...	6,321

CHAPTER XI.

ALTHOUGH no Rules for the construction of Iron Ships were promulgated by the Society till 1855, vessels of this description were admitted to classification in the Register Book at a much earlier date. The attention of the Society was first directed to iron as a material for ships about 1837, in which year the first iron vessel that received a class was built. This was the steamer *Sirius*, of 180 tons, built in London under the inspection of the Society's Surveyors, and owned at Marseilles. She appears in the supplement to the 1837 volume, having the A character without a term of years, and the notation "Built of iron." The next one entered in the Book was the iron sailing ship *Ironside*, of 270 tons, constructed in 1838 by Messrs. Jackson & Jordan, of Liverpool, for Messrs. Cairns & Co., of the same port. This vessel appears in the 1839 volume, with the same note "Built of iron," but without any class, although it is evident from the date, "11, 38," inserted in the column for classification, that she had been surveyed by the Society's officers in November, 1838.

From 1838 until 1844 the Committee continued to

record iron ships in the Register Book with no other designation than that of "built of iron," such as was accorded to the *Ironside*. In August, 1843, however, the Committee determined to collect all the evidence available from their surveying staff relating to the experiences acquired in regard to iron ships, and the Surveyors were requested to report to the Committee upon the qualities, durability of materials, workmanship, and fastenings of such vessels. These reports were duly received and considered by the Committee, and upon the 4th of January, 1844, a notice was issued that "in future (by a resolution passed that day) the character A 1 will be granted by the Society to vessels of iron built under the Survey of the Society's Surveyors, and reported to be of good and substantial materials and with good workmanship. All such vessels to be surveyed annually."

It should be added that before this date the number of iron ships had so increased, and the demand for some kind of higher class, based on fixed Rules, had become so general that the Committee appealed to the Shipbuilders of the country for assistance in compiling such Rules. This request was, however, made in vain, and the Iron Rules remained in a vague and indeterminate form until the year 1854. The Committee hesitated to lay down hard-and-fast lines for the construction of iron ships while such ships were in their infancy, preferring rather to await more lengthened experience.

During the next few years the reports received from the Surveyors stationed at all parts of the country constituted an excellent and safe guide in the preparation of the Rules for Iron Ships, when that task was at last undertaken.

Under the direction of Messrs. Martin and Ritchie, the Society's principal surveyors, every opportunity was taken for collecting trustworthy data in regard to the performances of iron ships. The principal iron Shipbuilders of the United Kingdom were also communicated with on the same subject, and the replies received from them proved in many cases of value to the principal surveyors in preparing their recommendations for the consideration of the Committee.

The earliest suggested Rules for Iron Ships of which any record exists were received from the Glasgow office of the Society, the Clyde being then, as now, one of the principal centres of the iron shipbuilding industry. They were dated the 10th of February, 1854, and were signed by Richard Robertson, Henry Adams, and Samuel Pretious, surveyors of the Society, stationed respectively at Glasgow, Hull, and Newcastle, who appear to have sat as a Committee upon the subject, by the direction of the Committee of the Register.

These proposals, slightly altered, appeared in the Register Book for 1855, in the form of the first Rules on Iron Shipbuilding issued by the Society, and were prefaced by the following remarks :—

> "Considering that Iron Shipbuilding is yet in its infancy, and that there are no well-understood general rules for building Iron Ships, the Committee have not deemed it desirable to frame a scheme compelling the adoption of a particular form or mode of construction; but that certain general requirements should be put for-

ward having for their basis thickness of plates and substance of frames, showing a *minimum in each particular*, to entitle ships to the character A for a period of years, subject, however, to certain periodical surveys; and also to a continuation of such character, should their state and condition justify it-on subsequent examination. For the purpose of attaining this object, the following Rules and the accompanying Table of Dimensions have been formed."

According to these Rules, iron ships built under survey might be classed for periods of twelve, nine, and six years, subject to occasional or annual surveys when practicable, and to a special survey in dry dock or on blocks every third year. The thickness of the plating, together with the spacing of the frames, determined the number of years assigned, there being a difference in thickness of 1-16th of an inch between each grade, and a difference in frame-spacing of two inches between the highest and the two lower grades; but in all other respects the requirements were common to the three classes. Following the provisions of the Rules for Wood Ships, one year was added to the period assigned in the case of vessels built under a roof; while vessels not surveyed during construction were classed A from year to year only, but for a period not exceeding six years.

On the expiration of the terms of classification, the vessels were liable to lapse to the Æ character, unless specially surveyed to determine their claims to be allowed a higher class.

The quantity of material used in iron ships at this period was considerable, as may be seen on reference to the scantlings and arrangements prescribed in the

Rules. For instance, the shell plating was required to be one inch in thickness for vessels of 3,000 tons of the highest grade, and the frames to be spaced not more than sixteen inches apart for the twelve-years' grade, this limit being increased to eighteen inches in vessels of the lower classes of nine and six years. In addition, all iron vessels were required to have a strake of clamp or ceiling plates fitted all fore and aft between the tiers of beams; and in vessels with only one tier of beams, the clamp was required to be fitted about two feet below the beams.

The foregoing Rules,—which underwent some alterations in 1857, when the thickness of the plating for vessels of the several grades was increased by 1-16th of an inch, and the frame-spacing was increased from sixteen to eighteen inches,—remained in force for nearly ten years, but they do not appear to have gained universal approval.

Mr. Ritchie, one of the Society's principal Surveyors, who took an active part in the preparation of the Rules for Iron Ships in 1854, has left upon record the following remarks in regard to them, which may now be read with interest and advantage:—

> "At the time the Committee drew up the first Rules in 1854, they felt that a classification of six, nine, and twelve years, although it might approach the truth as to the probable comparative durability of the various kinds of timber of which such ships were allowed by the Rules to be built, yet these characters could not correctly indicate the durability of vessels built of metal, which only deteriorated by the wasting of the surfaces, and whose durability depended upon different laws than that of timber."

It was considered, however, that these rules for classing would serve until more experience was gained, not only in the durability of iron when subjected to the continuous action of sea-water and the chemical action of some descriptions of cargoes, but also on unascertained points in the construction of iron ships which could not be premised from the most complete knowledge of wooden ships.

In the year following the preparation of the first Rules issued by the Society for the construction and classification of iron ships, the Committee passed resolutions sanctioning the continuation and restoration of such vessels, subject to their being submitted to certain prescribed examinations. The continuation granted upon the A character was not to exceed half the term assigned originally or on restoration, and the restoration could not exceed two-thirds the period originally assigned, and was to commence from the date of survey. Further resolutions were also adopted at the same time relating to vessels already classed without a term of years, by which such vessels might be granted a term, unless it should be found that, if they had been originally classed for a period of years, their characters would have expired, in which case they would lapse into the Æ class, if found entitled thereto.

In 1856 the Committee issued the very important regulation, that when the engines and boilers of iron ships were taken out of them, the ships should be submitted to a *particular and special survey*. The necessity for this measure has since been abundantly illustrated.

An important departure was taken about this time by admitting to classification vessels which were not built in accordance with the Society's Rules. In July, 1857, the Committee decided that ships built on peculiar principles should be specially surveyed every two years and marked " Expl. (B.S.)," denoting that they were of an experimental character, and were classed subject to their being surveyed biennially.

Mr. Ritchie said, in 1863, when addressing the Institution of Naval Architects :—" It should be borne in mind that, although the mode of constructing iron ships primarily intended by these Rules is the original ordinary one of vertical frames and longitudinal plating, the Committee do not hesitate to admit into the Register Book and into the same classes, vessels otherwise constructed, if of equal strength; and they have classed ships with longitudinal frames or with diagonal frames, and many with double or cellular bottoms for water-ballast." Contemporary evidence of this disposition of the Register Committee to afford every impetus in their power to constructive development is also obtainable from such an eminent shipbuilder as Mr. Scott Russell, the builder of the *Great Eastern*.

That gentleman, who built more novelties than any other shipbuilder of his time, when referring to this subject in 1860, alluded to "the *lex non scripta*, or unwritten Rule of Lloyd's"; and said that, although the Society was compelled to frame Rules for the guidance of its Surveyors, it was yet prepared to class a ship built in any other way, "if it can be shown that she is as strong as one built by the Rules"; and, further, that the Society "had relaxed their Rules in a way which enables them to combine with the strictness of Rules a defiance of any one saying that they stand in the way of the progress of iron shipbuilding." These statements are interesting now, as showing the hold which the Society had gained upon the goodwill and respect of the shipping community at a time when iron shipbuilding was in an unsettled and growing state, and when there were so many difficulties in the way of arriving at a just conclusion regarding the merits of the many modes of construction which were being proposed and tried.

CHAPTER XII.

WITH all the advantages that arose from the use of Iron for Shipbuilding, there was one objection which soon began to make itself apparent.

Experience showed that the bottoms of iron ships were more or less subject to fouling and corrosion, whereby the speed became greatly reduced after the vessels had been some few months at sea. Many attempts were made then, and have been continued since, to discover a material for coating the bottom which should prevent both fouling and corrosion; and, although some of the compositions in use do effect that result to a considerable degree, yet it must be admitted that to a large extent the same difficulty exists now as at the beginning.

Hence, so early as 1861, and even before then, various modes of sheathing the bottoms of iron ships were tried, the sheathing being in every case covered with copper or Muntz's metal; and ultimately the plating was in some instances entirely dispensed with, and wood planking wrought upon the iron frames. These latter vessels came to be spoken of as "Composite Vessels," and that designation is still retained. Their planking was, of course, caulked, and their bottoms were sheathed with copper or Muntz's metal, like those of ordinary wood ships, thus giving them all the advantages of the latter as to cleanliness and consequent speed.

The trade with China and the East Indies round the Cape of Good Hope created a special demand for vessels capable of making fast homeward passages, and the composite system was exactly adapted for such ships. The composite tea clippers, and their singularly swift ocean voyages, *viâ* the Cape, with cargoes of new teas, will long be remembered, although these ships are now becoming of the past, and the special work for which they were built is being performed by steamers.

The first composite ship to appear in the Register Book was the *Tubal Cain*, of 787 tons, which was entered in the edition for 1851 with the notation, " Iron frame, planked," and with the character A, but no term of years.

In 1860 and the immediately subsequent years this description of vessel appears to have been viewed with more favour than previously, as we find several shipbuilders inquiring what class the Committee would be prepared to give to such vessels when built. The experience of the Committee with this type of ship having led them to regard composite vessels as experimental, a notation to this effect was placed against these vessels in the Register Book, and they were subject to biennial survey, in order that particular attention might be paid to the condition of their fastenings.

Subsequent experience proved the wisdom of this course being adopted, as the renewal of bolt-fastenings has been the chief source of expense in the repairs of composite ships, except when entirely of copper or mixed metal. It was, however, at that time very doubtful whether the association of iron and copper in the framing and fastenings of these vessels would not lead to a galvanic action such as would result in the wasting of the former and the loosening of the latter. A term of years was, however, granted by the Committee, in accordance with the characters assigned to the wood materials employed in their construction, the same as in the case of wood ships.

Various modes of construction were at first proposed. Some of the vessels had wood floors and iron angle-frames; in others, the frames were of "channel" iron, or some equally novel sectional form; many variations also existed in the modes of fastening.

Under these circumstances, Mr. Waymouth, one of the Surveyors on the London establishment, proceeded, in 1864, by the Committee's direction, to prepare Rules for the construction of Composite ships, and these were adopted by the Committee, and issued as suggested Rules for Composite ships in the year 1867. As before, the period assigned was based upon the nature of the wood materials employed, and the character of the fastening,—an addition of one year being also given when the vessel was built under a roof. Indeed, the Rules were practically the same as those for wood ships so far as regards these points.

It should be stated that the Rules were illustrated with drawings prepared by Mr. Cornish, who is now one of the Assistants to the Chief Surveyor, and that the original drawings upon exhibition at Paris and Moscow were awarded Bronze and Gold Medals.

These Rules were universally adopted, and nearly every composite ship since built has been constructed in accordance with their provisions. Subsequent experience with these vessels has been very satisfactory, but the opening of the Suez Canal checked their production at once, especially as their construction is rather expensive, when compared with that of iron ships. Many of the composite ships still remain, doing good and regular service.

CHAPTER XIII.

AFTER the amalgamation of the Society with the Liverpool Register in 1845, no further change took place in the constitution of the Committee until 1863. But the intervening years were not allowed to pass without a renewal of the applications from the Provinces to be admitted to a share in the management of the Society. The enlargement of its London Board, by the admission of Nominees from Liverpool, touched the susceptibilities of the other outports; and the north-eastern districts, then rapidly growing in commercial activity, were not slow to take advantage of the opportunity thus afforded to urge their claims.

It was contended that the outports generally had a very insufficient voice in the management of the affairs of the Society; and that, as its operations extended to all the ports in the country, the election of the London Committee by and out of residents in the Metropolis was at variance with all principles of representation. These appeals, however, did not lead to any immediate result, and, as already stated, it was not till 1863 that any modification was made.

In that year the whole question of the representation of outports was raised by the Associations of Shipowners and Underwriters at Liverpool. The proposals of these bodies were brought under the consideration of the Committee at a special meeting on June 1st of that year, when it was resolved unanimously, that the Committee were prepared to consider favourably the proposition to admit additional Members, to be nominated from the outports. A deputation from Liverpool was received by the Committee in support of the views of the Shipping interests at that port, and at a subsequent meeting, specially convened, the following resolutions were adopted:—

> "That an addition, not exceeding ten Members, be made to the present Committee.
> "That four of the additional Members be nominated from Liverpool, viz., two to be elected by the Liverpool Shipowners' Association; two to be elected by the Liverpool Underwriters' Association."

It was left entirely to the discretion of the Associations above named to elect gentlemen who were or were not already Members of the Liverpool Committee; but in either case the Liverpool Committee, it was understood, should not be increased in the number of its Members.

The powers of the Liverpool Committee were at the same time somewhat enlarged, and a local Chairman of the Rotation Sub-Committee of Classification was appointed.

The remaining six additional Outport Members,

each of whom had to be either a Merchant, Shipowner, or Underwriter, were allotted as follows :—

Two Members for the Clyde—namely, one Underwriter, and one Shipowner.

One Merchant for the Tyne.

One Shipowner for the Wear.

One Merchant for Hull.

One Merchant for Bristol.

In the following year (1864) a further addition was made to the Committee in the person of a Member assigned to the Tees and Hartlepool district, and returnable as an Underwriter. This made the Members allotted to the north-eastern ports three in number—namely, a Merchant representing the Tyne, a Shipowner from the Wear, and an Underwriter elected on the Tees.

Regarding the admissibility of Shipbuilders as a constituent part of the Committee, it is interesting to observe what views were held on the subject by the Committee of that time. Touching a proposal received from Liverpool, to the effect that, besides the four additional Members allotted to that port, the Chairman for the time being of the Liverpool Shipbuilders' Association should be appointed a Member of the General Committee, the following resolutions were adopted :—

"That in readily acceding to the recommendation of the Liverpool Associations for the amendment of the Constitution of the Committee, by the admission of ten additional Representatives for the Outports, 'four of whom to be elected by the Shipowners and Underwriters of Liverpool, the residue to be distributed over the other

Outports, according to their importance,' this Committee were actuated by a sincere desire both to enlarge the sphere of usefulness of the Society, by a comprehensive extension of its administrative powers, and to give Liverpool the share of such power to which the extent of its interest in Maritime Commerce justly entitles it."

"That having already, in accordance with these principles, consented to the election from Liverpool, of the number of Representatives asked by the Liverpool Associations, this Committee cannot, in justice to the interests of other Outports, consent to any increase of that number, nor are they prepared, having reference to the original Constitution of the Society, and to all circumstances of the specific recommendation from Liverpool, to admit, as an element of the composition of the Superintending Authority, of a Representative of the Shipbuilding interest generally, and still less of a Representative of such interest from any one particular port."

"That this Committee are confirmed in the above Resolution from the consideration that the Liverpool Shipowners' Association, having the unrestricted right of selecting their own Representatives, have always the power of giving effect, should they see fit, to the objects of which they express approval."

Again, in the record of the proceedings attending the discussion of some proposals made on the northeast coast about this period, with the object of securing a local Committee of Reference, the following statement appears :—

"The Chairman [Mr. Chapman] explained to the Deputation that the Constitution of the Society required that the Committee should consist of Merchants, Shipowners, and Underwriters, in equal proportions, and that consequently the admission of Shipbuilders as an element in the Committee would be a violation of the Constitution on which the Society was formed."

The Committee of this Society have twice had under consideration the question of the advisability of an amalgamation with the "Underwriters' Registry for Iron Vessels," which was established in Liverpool in 1862.

The first occasion upon which the question arose was in 1870. In the early part of that year the Liverpool Branch Committee of this Society brought forward a proposal to the effect that some measures should be taken with a view to promote the closer association of the Steamship-owning Interest of the United Kingdom with the Register Book. This suggestion commending itself to the General Committee, a special Sub-Committee was then appointed to consider what steps could most properly be taken to secure the object. Liverpool being then the great centre of steam shipping, the Sub-Committee paid a visit to that port in August of the same year.

A basis of amalgamation between the Liverpool Registry and this Society was proposed, and was referred to a conference between the Special Sub-Committee, the Liverpool Branch Committee, and a Deputation from the Underwriters' Registry.

At this conference the subject was very fully discussed, but the propositions which were finally agreed upon did not commend themselves to the Committee of Lloyd's Register, to whose consideration they were submitted at a special meeting.

The question appears to have remained in abeyance until 1873, when it was revived by a Member of the General Committee of this Society.

Subsequently a meeting was arranged between delegates from each Society, and a report of their proceedings was considered by the General Committee of Lloyd's Register; but no further progress was made, and the proposal fell through.

In the meanwhile the Rules regulating the relations of the Liverpool Branch Committee with the London Board had undergone such revision as experience showed to be necessary; and under the arrangements then adopted, and which have remained in force unaltered up to the present time, the relations of the two Committees have been carried on with the most perfect harmony and with the most satisfactory results to all parties concerned.

The revised Code which was adopted in 1871 allowed Liverpool an additional member on the General Committee. In place of the representatives elected under the previous regulations by the Associations of Shipowners and Underwriters (who were not of necessity members of the Local Committee) and the three *ex-officio* members, it was determined that eight of the members of the Liverpool Committee should be members of the General Committee in London,—two to be elected by the Liverpool Shipowners' Association, two by the Liverpool Underwriters' Association, and the remaining four by the Liverpool Committee; two of the latter being the Chairman and Deputy Chairman, unless they should have been elected by either of the other electing Associations. It was at the same time decided to admit other members of the Liverpool Committee as substitutes for any of the eight Liverpool representatives who might be unable to attend a special meeting of the General Committee in London.

CHAPTER XIV.

IN the year 1863, after nine years' experience with the working of the Rules for building iron ships, the Committee again took this subject under their consideration, with a view to revision in those particulars which had been found to require it. As a preliminary measure, inquiries were made of the whole of the surveying staff and of the principal iron ship-builders in the United Kingdom, and replies were received from twenty-four Shipbuilders and twenty-eight Surveyors. The result of their recommendations, and the subsequent deliberations of the Committee, was a general revision of the Rules and an alteration in the mode of classification.

It had been found that the practice of classifying iron ships for terms of years was not in harmony with the characteristics of the material employed in their construction, which does not decay, but wastes on the surface by oxidation. The character of an iron ship would be determined by the thickness of the plates and angle-irons of which she is built—having regard to her dimensions and proportions. So long as these scantlings remain undiminished, or almost so, it is not reasonable that her character should suffer simply because she has reached a certain age. This was the opinion which had grown in the minds of the Society's officers during the course of their periodical examination of the iron ships classed in the Register.

The Committee therefore determined to class iron ships under the three grades, 100A1, 90A1, and A, and that these classes should be retained so long as the state of efficiency of vessels entitled them thereto. The 100A1 and 90A1 classes denoted vessels that had been built in accordance with, or equal to, the requirements of the Rules, while the A class consisted of vessels entitled to character A, but which had not been built according to the Rules. With the introduction of these new Rules, the frame-spacing was increased to twenty-one inches; but in vessels provided for half their length amidships with double frames, fitted back to back, and riveted to one another and to the floors and shell plating, the spacing could be extended to twenty-three inches. It was further resolved that, in order to ascertain the conditions of classed iron ships from time to time, they should be subjected to a special survey every four years in the 100A1 class, every three years in the 90A1 class, and every two years in the A class, in addition to the annual survey prescribed in the Rules in the case of every vessel.

These periodical special surveys now took the place of the continuation and restoration surveys previously required, and the Rules for these surveys were laid down with the same precision as those for reclassing wooden ships.

Many amendments were made in the Rules and

Tables of Scantlings previously in operation, but the number of these is too considerable for notice here. Their tendency was in the direction of reducing the scantlings towards the extremities of vessels, and in generally adjusting the proportions of the thicknesses of material in accordance with the strains and wasting influences to which they are subjected.

The attention given to this important question in 1863 marks an interesting epoch in the history of the Society, as the Rules then formulated constitute the groundwork of those in operation ever since.

The ample strength provided by the Rules for iron ships of the prevalent type of that day is clearly shown by the fact that many vessels built in accordance with them are still sound, and fit for the heaviest work.

The year 1870 witnessed a most important departure in the Rules for iron ships.

Up to that time the basis adopted in fixing the scantlings for iron ships under the Society's Rules was the under-deck tonnage, the same as that adopted in the cases of both wood and composite vessels. Experience, however, had shown that tonnage was not a suitable basis for regulating the scantlings of iron ships. Apart from other reasons, there was always the possibility of the limits of tonnage which fixed the scantlings of a vessel being exceeded. The tonnage could not be determined with certainty until the vessel was completed and measured by the Government officer; and in the case of vessels which it was intended should be slightly under any of the limits of tonnage, it not unfrequently occurred that when finished their tonnage was found to be in excess of those limits, thereby bringing the vessels under a higher scale of scantlings than that adopted in their construction. In such cases the Committee were unable consistently with their published Rules to assign to the vessels the classification contemplated.

Under these circumstances Mr. Waymouth, the present Secretary, who was then one of the principal Surveyors, submitted, as the result of the long and anxious thought he had given to the Rules, a proposal that the scantlings of iron vessels should be determined, not by their tonnage, but by certain of their dimensions. At the same time, he submitted new Rules and Tables, which had been framed by him on the proposed method. These Rules, which introduced for the first time the element of the proportion of breadth to length as affecting the scantlings of vessels, authorised a new and improved mode of construction, which, by the better distribution of the material in the structure, admitted of considerable reductions in the scantlings previously insisted upon.

In November, 1869, the first of a long series of meetings of a Sub-Committee was held to consider the Society's Rules for the construction and classification of iron ships. This Sub-Committee came to the conclusion that tonnage was not a proper standard for determining the scantlings of iron vessels. They, therefore, recommended that it should be abandoned, and that in place of it Mr. Waymouth's proposal and new Rules should be adopted.

It was in the first instance suggested that the

dimensions basis, referred to, should not be insisted upon generally, but should be sanctioned as an alternative standard, to be adopted at the option of the Shipbuilders, if they preferred it.

Mr. Waymouth's proposals, however, did not meet with the concurrence of Messrs. Martin and Ritchie, the principal Surveyors, who were strongly in favour of retaining the old method; and the Committee gave instructions for a conference to be held between them and some of the senior Surveyors from the outports. Several meetings took place, at which Mr. Martell, now the Chief Surveyor, took a leading part in combating the views of those opposed to Mr. Waymouth's suggestions, and after much discussion the opinions in favour of the alteration prevailed. Ultimately, as the result of a most careful and protracted consideration, the General Committee resolved to adopt the method proposed by Mr. Waymouth as the sole standard in determining the scantlings of iron vessels. The dimensions then adopted are such as those still in use for regulating the scantlings of iron ships in the present Rules.

With the new Rules the symbols 100A, 90A, 80A, &c., were introduced in the classification of iron ships. Vessels to which these classes are assigned are entitled to retain them so long as on survey they are found to be in satisfactory condition. Ships classed 100A to 90A inclusive are to be submitted to special survey every four years, while those classed 85A and under are to be specially surveyed every three years.

In 1871 the Rules for the construction of iron ships were still further revised, and Tables added, giving size of beams, breadth of stringer-plates, and particulars for the construction of iron and steel masts, bowsprits, and yards.

With some further modifications in the details, and additions where more recent experience has proved them to be necessary, the Rules passed in 1870 remain in force to this day. The basis of measurement is the same as was then adopted, and any changes which have been made are in the form of amendments in the scantlings.

CHAPTER XV.

WHILE the developments we have just recorded were being made in the Rules relating to iron ships, the Committee were not inactive in regard to those constructed of wood. The experience continually being acquired by the Surveyors pointed to the necessity for holding a special survey upon a vessel when half the period of her first classification, or continued or restored class had expired; and by a minute of the Committee in 1847 it was directed that, in addition to the ordinary annual surveys, a special survey should be held upon every vessel very soon after the expiration of one-half the period of her classification.

Various alterations were made about 1857. In that year the red A class was instituted, instead of the red *Æ, as the second description of the first class. Vessels not originally assigned a longer term than five years were not eligible for this class.

Under the provisions of the early Rules, vessels which were not submitted to survey for continuation or restoration on the expiration of their several terms of years on the A character, immediately lapsed to the Æ class. This was so far altered in 1857 that the word "lapsed" was set against ships in that condition, unless the owner requested the insertion of the Æ character; and the classification was omitted from the next reprint of the Register, unless the requisite survey had previously been held. The practice of inserting the word "expired" against vessels when they had run off the letter A was begun in 1863, and has continued to the present time.

About this period, also, was introduced the second survey, under the Rule for Continuation, already referred to as allowing an extension of two-thirds of the vessel's original term of years.

Other improvements of a somewhat earlier date were the regulations admitting ships classed A for short terms of years to the advantages of the continuation survey, and the special survey for A in red.

The special survey mark ✠, to indicate that a vessel has been surveyed specially and continuously during her construction, was first instituted in the year 1853. Continuous surveys were, of course, held for some time before a distinctive mark was chosen to indicate them; but it was only right that the great superiority of the conditions of survey in one case over the other should be properly recognised in the Register Book. The order was made retrospective, so as to apply to vessels already built and classed.

In 1865 a new character was introduced into the Register Book, foreign-built vessels, with scantlings not in accordance with the Rules, being classed 1 F, 2 F, or 3 F, according to their condition when surveyed. This character was continued in the book until 1876, when it was withdrawn, and owners of vessels of that class were requested to submit them to survey for some other character provided in the Rules.

The benefits arising from diagonal doubling of ships having been frequently brought under the notice of the Committee, they determined, in 1869, that ships should be allowed an extension of class, provided they were diagonally doubled when under survey for continuation on, or restoration to, the A class, or for the class of A in red. Vessels of the five-years' grade and under received two years' extension; those above five and under twelve years, three years' extension; while twelve-year ships had four years added to their time.

In 1871 it was further determined that any ships diagonally doubled, in accordance with the requirements of the Rules, would be eligible to receive a similar extension of time on the A class, provided they were not doubled before the expiration of twelve months from the date of launching. No vessel, which is allowed an extension of her original classification for doubling can have any further extension on the same ground when re-classed.

Several important alterations and additions to the Society's Rules for the classification of wooden vessels were made in the year 1870. Reference has already been made to the salting of ships—a beneficial practice which had by this time become frequent in some parts of the country. This was now made uniformly prevalent through the encouragement offered by the

Rules allowing an additional year in classification for salting.

The term of years assigned to certain descriptions of timber was also increased by the Committee in accordance with the latest experience acquired in regard to their durability. For instance, East India teak, which, until this time, had been classed as a twelve-years' material, was now raised to fourteen years. The periods assigned to certain other materials were at the same time reduced, in consequence of unfavourable reports regarding them. But the most important resolution adopted by the Committee relating to wood ships during the year 1870 is that known as the Mixed Material Rule.

The object of this new regulation, which was proposed by Mr. Waymouth, was to give to vessels built with mixed timber material (below the twelve-years' grade), of superior workmanship, and in which high-class material and extra fastenings had been judiciously employed to such an extent as to satisfy the Committee, an extension of class of not more than two years beyond that to which the lowest material used in their construction would otherwise entitle them. Through the operation of this Rule, encouragement was offered to the production of wood ships with the best materials and workmanship, and the owners of existing vessels of this description were to some extent remunerated for the extra outlay on their materials and fastenings.

In the year 1878 a further alteration was made in the Rules for wooden ships by raising the grade of certain materials, especially when salted, it having been found that American oak and fir timber were worthy of a higher character when salted than had been hitherto assigned to them. The periods allowed for other materials were lowered, and some woods were wholly expunged from the Table.

Very few wood vessels are, however, now being built, iron and steel having almost entirely superseded the once universal material for ships. But there can be little doubt that wood ships were never better built than when they were being superseded by iron vessels.

The figure 2, representing a defective equipment, was withdrawn in 1876, and the mark, thus — substituted. In the same year the I, or lowest character, was omitted from the Rules and Register Book.

CHAPTER XVI.

ALTHOUGH, from the commencement of the Society's existence, it was styled a Register of British and Foreign Shipping, yet for many years afterwards there was no provision made for the survey of ships abroad. Applications had been made at different times for appointment to the post of Surveyor at one or other of the principal foreign seaports, but the Committee had never acceded thereto.

From a very early period in the history of British North America and the United States, ship-building was an important industry, being, doubtless, fostered by the abundance and cheapness of the fir and oak timber on the uncleared lands. And, although the oaks were inferior to those of the West of Europe, and the firs no more durable than such timber is anywhere, yet, as the available dimensions were considerable, the deficiency in strength and durability was largely compensated for by the extra scantlings employed.

The earliest statistics published by the Society show that the number of new vessels built in the " British Plantations," as they were termed, was by no means small, even when compared with those built in this country. The modes of construction were not, however, very good. Men who tilled the land in the summer addressed themselves to shipbuilding during the hard Canadian winter, when agricultural operations were necessarily at a standstill. There was consequently a great need for skilled supervision in the construction of these vessels, and so early as 1851 a letter was received by the Secretary from St. John, New Brunswick, stating that the written authority and guarantee of several respectable shipowners in St. John had been given for the sum of £300 a year during five years, as a basis for the appointment of a Surveyor to the Society at that port.

It soon became apparent that in the North American Colonies there was a wide field for the Society's usefulness. In 1852 a Surveyor was appointed for Quebec and the River St. Lawrence, and in the following year another officer was placed at St. John, New Brunswick. These appointments were quickly followed by others. Two Assistant-Surveyors, one for each port, were sent out within the next two years; and when, in the course of two more years, these officers were assigned separate districts of their own,—one becoming Surveyor of a newly-opened surveying district at Prince Edward Island, and the other being allotted the Miramichi district,— the vacancies caused by their removal were filled up by additional appointments, thus making no less than six Surveyors to the Society stationed in North America.

In 1856 the Committee appointed a Surveyor for Holland and Belgium, and selected for the office Mr. Pretious, already on the Society's staff, who remained until 1861, when he was recalled.

No further steps towards the appointment of Surveyors on the Continent seem to have been taken until 1866, when Mr. L. Meyer was appointed as Surveyor for Holland and Belgium, residing at Antwerp.

Early in the year 1868 a memorial, forwarded by thirty merchants and shipowners in Holland, was received by the Committee, suggesting the appointment of a resident Surveyor at Rotterdam. Six months afterwards Mr. Meyer recommended that the deputies or agents appointed by him at Amsterdam, Rotterdam, and Veendam, should be appointed Assistant-Surveyors. In January, 1869, this recommendation was acted upon, and, shortly after, these assistants were made independent officers.

Earlier in the same year an English Surveyor was sent out to Shanghai as the Society's officer, he being the first representative of the Register on the continent of Asia. In the following year Surveyors were appointed at Trieste, Ancona, and Venice. The succeeding year, 1871, saw Surveyors representing the Society established at Bordeaux, Hamburg, Melbourne, and Sydney; and in 1872 similar appointments were made at Copenhagen, Bergen, and Genoa.

In 1872, Mr. Waymouth visited Genoa and inspected the vessels building there. Upon his return, he reported to the Committee that he had found a large quantity of shipbuilding in progress at that port, and on his recommendation one of the Surveyors on the London staff was associated with the local Surveyor.

At that time wood, and even iron shipbuilding—but especially the former—was in an active condition at the Italian ports. The materials for wood ship construction were both good and abundant, but the system of fastening was defective. It was extremely necessary, therefore, that the supervision of a Surveyor trained in the English practice should be given in the application of the Society's Rules in the Italian and Austrian ports.

Additions to the number of the foreign Surveyors have been made from time to time, as the necessity for their appointment became apparent; so that, whilst in 1870 there were five officers of this class, in 1873 the number had risen to twenty-two. At the present time there are no fewer than sixty-six non-exclusive Surveyors abroad; and the Society may now be considered fairly represented in all parts of the globe.

CHAPTER XVII.

IT will have been observed that the system of classification adopted even by the earliest Registers took cognisance of the state of a vessel's equipment, the relative efficiency being recorded with the character assigned to the hull.

In 1834, when this Society was established, the Rules merely specified the number of anchors and the length of cable required for different sized vessels. This was supplemented in 1846 by the issue of instructions to the Surveyors, to see that all new chains supplied to classed vessels had been duly tested, and the strain marked on each length.

In 1853 it was made imperative that certificates of test should be produced previously to the vessels being classed.

Five years later, the Committee issued the present Table No. 22, showing the number and weight of anchors, and length and size of cables, hawsers, and warps for various sizes of sailing vessels and steamers. The Committee decided, at the same time, to allow a reduction to be made in the sizes of chain cables which satisfactorily withstood the Admiralty test at a public proving-machine.

In 1862 the Committee introduced the Rule requiring all anchors and chain cables supplied for vessels, classed or proposed for classification in the Society's Register Book, to be tested and certified at a public machine, and in the same year at great cost they established the Society's Proving House at Poplar for the testing of chains and anchors. This establishment was abandoned by the Society in 1873, on account of the great expense it entailed. It was then leased by the Trinity House, who kept it open till 1875, when it was finally closed and the plant disposed of.

The Committee's requirements were made more stringent in 1863, by the addition of a proviso that no testing would be recognised unless done at an establishment belonging to a Corporation or open to an Inspector appointed by, and under the entire control of, Lloyd's Register; but these regulations did not come into full operation till 1864. This arrangement continued for some years.

In 1871, the Laws respecting the proving and sale of chain cables and anchors were amended by an Act of Parliament, under which licences could be granted by the Board of Trade only to certain corporations or public bodies. Under this Act the testing certificates of the several joint-stock Companies owning Proving Houses could not be recognised. Consequently, the Committee, at the suggestion of the Board of Trade and with the consent of the Proprietors, agreed to undertake the sole control of the testing operations at such establishments. The licences for these works are granted to the Committee, who appoint a General

Superintendent and also local Superintendents of Testing.

The superintendence of the Committee has within recent years been extended to several Proving Houses previously under the management of Corporations or public bodies; until at the present moment all but one of these Proving Establishments are under the control of the Society.

CHAPTER XVIII.

IT has already been stated that in the early days of steam vessels the Committee were satisfied, so far as the machinery and boilers of classed vessels were concerned, with receiving a report of their efficiency from a recognised competent Marine Engineer.

The Rules issued in 1834 contained the following provisions:—

> "All seagoing Vessels navigated by *Steam* shall be required to be surveyed *twice in each Year*, when a character shall be assigned to them according to the report of survey as regards the classification of the hull and materials of the vessel.
>
> "With respect to the Boilers and Machinery, the Owners are required to produce to the Surveyors to this Society, at the above-directed surveys, a certificate from some competent *Master Engineer*, describing their state and condition at those periods."

The machinery so certified was to be described by the letters "M.C." in the Register Book; but if no certificate of the condition of the engines and boilers were furnished as directed, then no character could be assigned.

A few years later the public mind was agitated by the serious loss of life which not infrequently occurred in connexion with boiler explosions on board ship, and steps were therefore taken by the Committee to secure a more rigid compliance with the Rules, quoted above, for the survey of steam vessels.

This was the beginning of the Machinery Surveys which now constitute so important a feature in the Society's operations. Although duly appointed Engineer Surveyors to the Society were not employed till within recent years, it is interesting to observe that an application for the post of Engineer Surveyor was received by the Committee as far back as the year 1838.

In 1873, however, the number of steam vessels had increased so largely, that the Committee felt they would be no longer justified in classing them, without taking steps to assure themselves with the same certainty as in the case of the hulls of the vessels that the whole of the details of the machinery were in thoroughly safe condition. Accordingly, after the matter had been carefully considered by a Sub-Committee nominated for the purpose, the Committee, in January, 1874, decided to augment their surveying staff by appointing Engineer Surveyors.

At the outset they were fortunate in securing the services of Mr. William Parker as Chief Engineer Surveyor, and, at the same time, they appointed as Ship and Engineer Surveyors two gentlemen who were experienced Marine Engineers. Within twelve months four other Engineer Surveyors were appointed.

Since that time, as this branch of the Society's usefulness has developed, the staff has been gradually increased, until at the present time it consists of one Chief Engineer Surveyor, with two assistants, twenty Engineer Surveyors, and seven Ship and Engineer Surveyors, all of whom are exclusively the servants of the Society, while there are also ten Engineer Surveyors and sixteen Ship and Engineer Surveyors stationed in foreign ports who are not employed solely by the Society.

One of the earliest subjects to which the attention of the Engineer Surveyors was drawn was the comparatively simple, but very important, matter of the arrangement of sea cocks and pipes in connexion with the engines. In a large percentage of vessels, these were found to be so arranged that by carelessness on the part of the engineers or firemen the cocks could be made to open a direct communication between the sea and the engine-room. This was so evidently a source of great danger to the vessel, that in all cases, as soon as the faulty arrangements were pointed out to the shipowners, they took steps to have them altered. There can be no doubt that this simple matter of faulty arrangement of pipes had previously been the cause of many mysterious founderings of steam vessels, while some vessels had even sunk from this cause when in dock.

Those Engineer Surveyors who were stationed at ports where engines and boilers were being constructed for vessels intended for classification, examined them during construction, and reported in full detail the scantlings of the various parts of the machinery and boilers; so that the Committee were early in possession of the practice of the principal Marine Engineers of the country, and by obtaining similar information in the cases of old vessels, in which the machinery had been proved by experience to be sufficient, they were soon able to formulate Rules for the strength of boilers, and these Rules immediately obtained the confidence of manufacturing Marine Engineers. They have since, of course, been slightly modified from time to time, in accordance with the teachings of experience, or as the advancement of Engineering has introduced new conditions of construction.

Although the Society's Rules are applicable to the existing practice of marine engineering, in no case have they been allowed to interfere with the introduction of improved methods of construction or application. The Rules, while so framed as to insure strength and safety in all respects, place no restriction upon the design or proportions of engines, and therefore afford free scope for the skill and inventive ingenuity of the country.

As regards novelties in engineering, it is the practice of the Committee in every case, before deciding upon a new departure, to carefully investigate the matter. When they are assured that ample safety is provided, the arrangement is sanctioned unconditionally; if the plan is such as to require further experience to prove its durability, or if the arrangement is of such a nature that its efficiency depends greatly upon increased attention being bestowed upon it, approval is given conditionally upon its being subject to frequent surveys; and only in the event of the proposal being altogether unsuitable would the Committee disallow it. This elasticity in the Rules which govern the Society's inspection of machinery has been greatly taken advantage of by enterprising engineers and shipowners.

When the survey of machinery was first undertaken, the supervision, although sufficient in the main to ensure soundness of materials and good workmanship, was not of so thorough and minute a description as that at present exercised. Very soon, however, shipowners found its value, and made special requests for the Engineer Surveyors to pay particular attention to the details of engines building for them, and expressed their readiness to pay extra fees for the extra services they required. On consideration, the Committee sanctioned these surveys, the enginemakers in every case being perfectly willing, not only to allow such inspection to be made, but also to carefully consider any suggestions made by the Surveyors as to matters of detail which would, if carried out, be likely to add to the durability and efficiency of the machinery.

This special supervision became so much appreciated, and necessitated so much additional labour on the part of the Surveyors, that the Committee, on enlarging the Engineering staff, thought that general satisfaction would be given by requiring that the machinery of all steam vessels built under special survey should be also constructed under special survey; and this requirement has been found to work so well, that at the present time not only is the machinery for all new vessels intended for classification built under special survey, but practically also all the renewals, both of engines and boilers, are carried out under special survey; whilst engines and boilers building for stock by several makers are now being specially surveyed during construction.

Not the least important, and certainly by far the most arduous, duty of the Engineer Surveyors is that of the periodical surveys required to be held on the machinery of classed vessels.

At each of the special surveys of steam vessels, the machinery and boilers have to be carefully examined in all important working parts; and in addition to these surveys, the boilers are also subjected to special survey at shorter intervals, according to their age. After the boilers of a vessel are four years of age they are not allowed to run without re-survey for a longer period than two years, while after they are six years old they are required to be surveyed at least every year.

To show the extent of the work undertaken by this branch of the Society, it will perhaps suffice to state that in August, 1878, there were 246 sets of engines and boilers being constructed under special survey. In the same month in 1879 there were 126, in 1880 there were 292, in 1881 there were 401, in 1882 there were 456, and in 1883 there were 424. Besides these, there are at all times a large number of new boilers being made to replace those worn out in old vessels.

CHAPTER XIX.

THE improvements in the manufacture of steel previously to the year 1860 led to attempts being made by several Shipbuilders to employ that material in the construction of ships. But the processes were not sufficiently perfected at the time to produce steel of a uniform and trustworthy character, fit for the purposes of the Shipbuilder and Shipowner. In 1862 applications were made for vessels to be classed which were about to be built of puddled steel; but the Committee replied, that in the absence of experience regarding the durability of steel it was not in their power to sanction the proposal.

In the case of a steam yacht of 2,400 tons built for the Viceroy of Egypt in 1864, under the survey of the Society's Surveyors, and constructed partly of steel, the Committee consented to a reduction being made in the steel scantlings, amounting to about one-fourth of the thicknesses allowed in an iron ship of the same size. In 1866 plans were submitted for building a vessel of 1,552 tons with Barrow hematite steel, the sectional area of the material to be two-thirds that required by the Rules for a similar vessel if built of iron. Upon this proposal, the Committee decided, on certain conditions, to class the vessel on completion as " Experimental."

In 1867 a report was made to the Committee by some of the principal Surveyors to the Society, upon the steel manufactured at Barrow-in-Furness, by the Bessemer process. Having considered this report, the Committee agreed to class ships built under special survey of steel of approved quality. The notation " Experimental " was, however, to be made against the characters of such vessels in the Register Book. A reduction was allowed in the thickness of the plates, frames, &c., of ships built of steel, not exceeding one-fourth the thickness prescribed for iron ships. It was required that the steel should be able to withstand a tensile strain of not less than 30 tons to the square inch. This appears to be the first occasion upon which tests were applied to steel, so as to enable the Committee to formulate regulations for its use in classed ships.

Further tests were made early in the following year upon steel manufactured at Bolton-le-Moors, but the results were not so satisfactory, the report stating that the quality of the steel would not warrant the Surveyors in recommending it for any reduction in scantling from that allowed for iron of good quality.

Several years were allowed to elapse before the question of the suitability of steel for shipbuilding purposes again occupied public attention. About the year 1877 there occurred what has not inaptly been termed the " resurrection " of steel.

The objections made to steel during the earlier days of its manufacture were two-fold. In the first place, the material was of a hard, brittle, and untrustworthy character; whilst, even if the quality of the metal had been above reproach, the price was quite beyond that which would have enabled it to enter into competition with iron.

During the interval between 1867 and 1877, however, great changes had taken place. Improvements had been made in the manufacture of steel by the Bessemer process, and a new method of manufacture, viz., the Siemens-Martin or open-hearth process, had been introduced. The production, at a greatly reduced cost, of a mild and ductile material differing from iron only in being superior to it was thus rendered possible, and the present development of the use of mild steel for the construction of ships and boilers may be dated from this time.

A review of the action of the Society in this matter will show that the careful investigations made by the Society's Officers, and the subsequent approval of the material by the Committee, had the effect of largely aiding its introduction by giving the public confidence in its suitability for the purposes intended.

The first proposal to use this new steel for classed vessels was made by Messrs. John Elder & Co., of Glasgow, who, in 1877, commenced to build two paddle-steamers of that material, under the survey of the Society's officers, to the order of the London, Brighton, and South Coast Railway Company. In the same year the Wallsend Slipway Company, of Newcastle, submitted a plan of the first marine boiler proposed to be made entirely of steel. Before giving their approval in these cases, the Committee required a series of tests to be applied to the material intended for use in the structures, in order to ascertain its suitability. In the case of the boiler, tests were also applied, in order to ascertain the actual strength of the flat plates stayed as proposed, and of the riveted seams of its shell.

At the same time the Society's professional advisers visited the principal steel manufactories in the kingdom, as also the principal establishments where steel had been used for boiler purposes, the material having already by this time come into very extended use for locomotive and stationary boilers.

At each of these places information was gained as to the properties of the material and the conditions required to be complied with in working it in order to insure satisfactory results. The information gained was freely placed at the disposal of all interested in the subject; and so much confidence in the material was the result, that it became freely used for both shipbuilding and boiler-making. In the case of boilers, it was used in many parts for which the most expensive brands of iron before had been exclusively employed.

During the earlier periods of its use there were a few failures of steel plates, which had at first a mysterious appearance, and which would undoubtedly have thrown so much suspicion upon the material, unless they had been promptly and exhaustively investigated, and their true cause discovered, that its use would have been seriously retarded. The causes of failure were in each instance investigated by the Society's officers, and were clearly traced to faulty manipulation, and not to defective material. Increased experience with steel has, however, led to its properties being better understood, and the Engineer and the Shipbuilder are enabled to handle it now without fear of such failures occurring.

One great cause of the confidence which is felt in mild steel is no doubt the fact that the steel plates are all tested before leaving the manufactory, and are required to be capable of withstanding certain specified tests. These tests are witnessed by the Society's Surveyors, and they are so comprehensive that material which will withstand them can with confidence be used for any part of a ship or boiler.

The result of the use of steel in shipbuilding is a general reduction of 20 per cent. below the scantlings prescribed in the Rules for Iron Ships. In the case of boilers, in which a reduction is also allowed in the thickness of the shell plating and stays, there ensued a great increase of steam pressures. Ten years ago the common steam pressure in new boilers was from 60 lb. to 65 lb. per square inch, 75 lb. being then looked upon as very high.

These limits of pressure were arrived at by reason of the difficulty of properly working the thick boiler shell plates which higher pressures would have necessitated. The use of steel of greater strength than iron admits of the same thickness of plates being sufficient for much higher pressures, and now very few boilers for new engines are constructed to carry a less working pressure than 90 lb. per square inch, while very many are made to work at 150 lb. per square inch.

These increased pressures result in a greater economy of fuel consumption than is possible with lower pressures.

The increase in the use of steel for shipbuilding during recent years is shown by the following account of the amount of the tonnage built of steel under the Society's inspection :—

Year.	Tonnage of Steel Ships.	Steel Steamers.	Total Tonnage.
1880	1,342	34,031	35,373
1881	3,167	39,240	42,407
1882	12,477	113,364	125,841
1883	15,703	150,725	166,428

*   *   *   *

About two years ago, another departure occupied the attention of the Society's principal officers. Steel-makers had so far improved upon the methods used for making heavy steel castings that they stated these could now be made more trustworthy than heavy iron forgings, both for engine work and stern and rudder frames.

The processes of making these castings were specially investigated, and the quality of the resulting material was ascertained, and several of the various articles which had been manufactured were tested to destruction. As a result, the use of these castings has been sanctioned by the Committee for crank-shafts and several other important parts of engines, and also for stern-frames, rudders, and rudder-frames. In order that these castings may be accepted, it is necessary that they shall be found to be sound and free from blow-holes, and that test pieces cast with them shall be found by actual test to have a tensile strength of not more than thirty tons per square inch. It is also required that other test pieces, cast on them and planed to an inch and a quarter square, shall bend cold without fracture through an angle of 90 degrees over a circular arc having a radius not greater than an inch and three quarters. These tests are so severe that none but material of great ductility can withstand them. The whole of the shafts, frames, &c., which have been approved of by the Society upon these conditions have so far given satisfaction, and have justified the confidence reposed in them.

The results of all tests upon steel for shafts, frames, &c., as well as those made on a large number of riveted joints of steel plates, have been freely published, together with other matters of interest to Shipbuilders and Engineers, by means of official reports and of papers read at the various Technical Institutions; and in this way much good has no doubt been done in disseminating useful knowledge regarding the capabilities of the new materials and the most approved methods of manipulating them.

*   *   *   *

The appointment in 1882 of Inspectors of Forgings may be mentioned as a more recent extension of the Society's operations. Previous to that time large forgings intended for classed vessels were inspected after delivery at the shipbuilding or engineering establishment in a finished state.

Experience had shown, however, that serious defects might exist in Forgings, which it would be impossible to discover by an examination of them when finished, while it had also been found that the methods adopted in welding large forgings were in many instances open to much objection. With a view to the improvement of the methods of construction, and to the prevention, so far as possible, of the use of defective forgings, the Committee decided to appoint Officers who, from their special training, should possess the qualifications necessary for the careful inspection of all large forgings during the process of manufacture.

CHAPTER XX.

UPON the opening of the Royal School of Naval Architecture and Marine Engineering at South Kensington in 1864, provision was made for the training there of students from private establishments. Few, however, availed themselves of the opportunity thus offered for obtaining a scientific acquaintance with the principles of their profession, and as a consequence the educational resources of the School were chiefly devoted to the training of Admiralty students. The transfer of the school to the Royal Naval College at Greenwich in 1873 did not make any difference in this respect; and, as it was yearly becoming a matter of greater importance that the theoretical principles of Naval Architecture and Marine Engineering should be more carefully studied in Shipbuilding and Marine Engineering establishments, the Committee of the Society resolved in 1877 to grant the sum of £100 per annum towards the maintenance of two private students at the College, viz., one in Naval Architecture and one in Marine Engineering.

In 1878 the grant was increased to £150 per annum, in order to establish an annual scholarship of

£50 a year, tenable for three years, to be competed for by private students of Naval Architecture or Marine Engineering at the Royal Naval College. The Lords Commissioners of the Admiralty, who had also founded a similar scholarship, accepted this offer of the Committee, and issued regulations as to the competition. Only British subjects are eligible, and the candidates have to undergo a competitive examination in mathematics and the principles of their profession.

It is to be regretted that no candidates have proved themselves to be qualified for either the Admiralty or Lloyd's Scholarship. The Committee have at different times appointed graduates of the Royal Naval College as Surveyors to the Society, and at the present time there are nine of the Society's Surveyors in different parts of the kingdom who were trained at that institution.

CHAPTER XXI.

IN 1877 the Committee, upon the invitation of a number of leading Yacht Owners and Builders, undertook the special classification of yachts, and issued Rules and Regulations for their construction. The necessity for a system of classification for yachts similar to that which had been applied so long, and with such satisfactory results, to merchant ships, suggested itself to gentlemen specially interested in yachting. Classes had been assigned for many years prior to that date to yachts which had been built in accordance with the Society's Regulations for the construction of merchant vessels; but it is obvious those Regulations were not suited to vessels of the former description.

The matter did not, however, take any definite shape until 1877, when, through the instrumentality of Mr. Dixon Kemp, a Committee of Yacht Owners and Builders was formed, with the object of taking steps to institute a Yachting Registry. It was ultimately decided that advantage should be taken of the existing organisation and staff of Lloyd's Register, and the Committee of this Society consented to undertake the

YACHT REGISTER.

1884-85

1 Official Number. Internation'l Code Signal Letters.	2 Yachts' Names, &c.	3 Rig. Sailmakers' Names.	4 TONS. Registered Net & Gross / Thames Measurmnt	5 DIMENSIONS. Registered or Thames Measurement Length / Br'dth / Depth	6 Engines of Steamers. Builders of Engines. Materials, Repairs of Vessels, &c., if Classed.	7 BUILD. Builders. / Designers.	8 Where. / When.	9 Owners.	10 Port belonging to.	11 Port of Survey.	12 Year if Assigned
	Thistle Iron 7B.11ds 3Masts Cem.81		90.9·80 69·07 2Dks 44	186·95 25·15 14·1 *Roof*	C.I.2Cy.26″ & 52″—33″ 80lb. 112HP. *Blackwd & Gordon, P.Gls*	Blackwood & Gordon / *Blackwood & Gordon*	Pt.Glasgw 1881 6mo.	Duke of Hamilton, KT	London	Lloyd's	
	Thistle C,5,81C.F.		17	54·0 12·0 9·9 *Roof*		Stow & Son / *Dixon Kemp*	Shoreham 1881 5mo.	W. Orr Ewing	Greenock	Lloyd's	
	Thistle			21·0 8·0		Goodall	St.Helen's I.W. 1870	W. Murdoch	Lyningt'n		
	Thora C.7,80c.f.			66·6 13·3 ·8 *Beams part Chestnut*	10 & 12yrs Mat.	Fife & Son / *W. Fife, sen.*	Fairlie 1880 5mo.	John Ferguson	Greenock		
	Thought			50·9 11·3 8·5 *alt.53 by Hatcher*		J. Harvey & Wivenhoe / *J. Harvey*	1852	Maj. Harlowe-Turner	Falmouth		
	Thought			30·0 8·2		Bevan	Swansea 1873	Charles Gold	Swansea		
	Thought			28·5 7·0 4·7		H. Totam / *H.Totam*	Queenst'n 1876	Capt. James Beatty	Queenst'n		
	Thyra 3Masts (late Elabeth) Iron 5B.11ds Ccm.—		106·4 15·4 len.20ft.81 by White, Cowes	7·9 C.I.2Cy.16″ & 26″–18″ 20HP. *J.Penn & Son, London*		A.D. Lewis & Co.	London 1876	Delabere P. Blaine s.s.Cws.No.1-81-4yrs	London		
	Thyra			47·7 9·96 6·8		Fife & Son / *W.Fife & Son*	Fairlie 1875	Archibald Colville	Glasgow		
	Tiercel C.79 C.F.			79·8 18·7 10·3 12 & 16yrs Mat. *Roof*		Camper & Nicholson	Gosport 1868	W. F. Stutfield	Prtsmouth	H.T.Gos.79	

duty. A Register Book, devoted exclusively to this description of vessel, has since been issued annually, and has met with a large measure of success, the Subscribers thereto, who numbered about 320 on the first issue of the volume, having risen to nearly 1,000 within the space of six years. The Book contains very full particulars of all British Yachts from the largest to the smallest, whether classed or not, and, as much information as can be obtained of those owned abroad; also a list of British and Foreign Yacht Clubs, and coloured plates illustrative of their respective Flags, an index of Signal Letters, and an alphabetical list of the names and addresses of the owners.

Owners have largely availed themselves of the advantages of classification of yachts by the Society, no less than about 600 vessels having come under the inspection of the Society's Surveyors since the institution of the Yacht Register. The symbols of classification are similar to those employed in the classing of merchant ships. The Rules provide for the construction and periodical examination of wood, iron, and composite Yachts.

As another indication of the tendency of the Society's operations to spread beyond the limits of ordinary sea-going Mercantile Shipping, attention may be called to the frequent requests which have been made during late years for the Survey and Classification of Fishing-smacks, Trawlers, &c., to which vessels a particular class, " for fishing purposes," has been assigned.

CHAPTER XXII.

IT has already been remarked that a column containing "the feet of the draught of water when loaded" was inserted in the third earliest copy of a Register Book, dated 1774-75-76, and this column was continued down to the time of the establishment of Lloyd's Register on its present basis in 1834. No information is obtainable as to how and by whom the load-draught was determined; but, as the draught is given in all cases in round numbers, it appears probable that it was furnished, not with the object of placing any limit on the loading, but rather as an index to the size of the vessels.

On the institution of this Society in 1834, the record of draught of water was not inserted in the Register Book, and no step appears to have been taken by the Society in connexion with the subject of the load-line until 1870. In that year, on the introduction into the Rules of provision for the construction of vessels of the awning-decked type to meet the requirements of trade, such vessels were required, in order to prevent overloading, to have scuppers through the sides, and ports to discharge water at the main deck, so that in no case could they be laden to the level of that deck. In some instances, however, the ports and scuppers at the main deck were permanently closed by the Owners, to enable the vessels to be loaded deeper. Upon this fact becoming known to the Committee, they determined, in February, 1873, to suspend the characters of all awning-decked vessels having the main-deck scuppers closed.

In August of the same year the scuppers in such vessels were allowed to be closed, provided a load-draught agreed to by the Committee were inserted in the Register Book and on the Certificate; and, in the Rules issued in 1874, the load-line was made compulsory for all new awning-decked vessels. As the practice of closing the scuppers at the main deck, without a fixed load-line being assigned, still continued, the Committee, in December of the following year, resolved that a load-line should be determined by the Society for every awning-decked vessel classed in the Register Book. This decision was followed by the requirement that a diamond-shaped mark, with the letters L, R, placed one on either side of it, should be painted on the vessel's sides at the draught approved by the Committee.

So important a step as the enforcement of a fixed load-line, retrospective in its action, was not allowed to pass unchallenged. A well-known firm of ship-owners, owning several vessels of the awning-decked type, declined to comply with the Committee's requirements; and, on the characters of their vessels being expunged from the Register Book, they commenced a test-action against the Society in respect of one of them, damages being laid at £1,000. The case was decided in the Society's favour upon all material points. In summing up, the Judge observed that —

> "The Pursuers' case depends on the validity of their proposition, that the facts averred by them imply a contract between them and the Defenders with respect to the . . . . whereby the classification of that vessel on the Register shall be preserved so long as the Rules and Regulations of the Association in force at the date of the original registration in 1872 are complied with. I cannot sustain this proposition."

And added that—

> "It would be a grave misfortune, and greatly impair public confidence in the Association, if a Court of Law were to hold that they were under implied contract with respect to all ships already classified which compelled them to continue the classification after they had become satisfied that it was undeserved, and therefore misleading."

The judgment was appealed against, but was upheld, on appeal. The right of the Committee to make such alterations in the Society's Rules as experience may show to be necessary, and to apply the same retrospectively, was thereby fully established.

The importance of this decision, as affecting the freedom of action of the Society, cannot be overestimated. It is, perhaps, not too much to say that, had the verdict been for the Pursuers, the Society's influence for good upon the Mercantile Marine would have been greatly curtailed.

In the issue of the Society's Rules in 1870, which contained for the first time a reference to awning-decked vessels, provision was also made for the construction of spar-decked vessels "for passengers only." No scuppers were required to be fitted to the main deck of these vessels, but the freeboard considered suitable was indicated. This freeboard was, however, in no sense compulsory, and the Rule disappeared in the following year, when the description of vessel to which it was applicable ceased to be constructed.

In the meantime, while the Society had been taking steps to prevent improper loading of awning-decked vessels, the Board of Trade obtained powers from Parliament to detain overladen vessels as unseaworthy, and in November, 1875, the Board applied to the Committee for assistance in laying down elementary principles concerning freeboard and draught of water. Representatives were eventually appointed, and a Committee formed, consisting of nominees of the Society, of the Board of Trade, and of the Liverpool Underwriters' Registry.

The Committee met, but it did not appear that opinions upon the subject of a load-line for all vessels were so matured as to give the hope of an agreement being arrived at by its members, and the Committee was accordingly dissolved.

Among the members of Lloyd's Register Committee, however, a growing desire was manifested to grapple with this intricate subject, and many discussions took place regarding it. They ultimately arrived at the conclusion that a certain percentage of surplus buoyancy for each particular ship would form the proper basis for a load-line. To ascertain the practice in regard to loading vessels in this country, the Society's Surveyors were instructed to take note of the immersion of vessels at the various ports, and their reports upon the subject were duly forwarded to the Committee. At the request of the Committee, many of the principal shipowners furnished particulars of the draughts to which they loaded their vessels. This information was being accumulated for a considerable time preparatory to its being analysed, with a view to the construction of Tables of Freeboard, when in August, 1880, the Board of Trade inquired of the Committee whether the measures adopted for fixing a conditional load-line for awning-decked ships could with propriety be extended to other classes of vessels.

The Committee, having by this time received much valuable information from their Surveyors and the Shipowners with whom they had communicated, and having besides in their sole possession full particulars of the strength and mode of construction of the various vessels, instructed Mr. Martell, the Chief Surveyor, to frame Tables of Freeboard suitable for every type of vessel.

Mr. Martell, who had already given much attention to this subject, and had, so long before as 1873, prepared Tables of Freeboard, based upon the principle of reserve buoyancy, which he laid before the Royal Commission on Unseaworthy Ships, proceeded to give effect to the Committee's instructions. So laborious, however, was the undertaking, it was not until January, 1882, that the information obtained had been exhaustively analysed and preliminary Tables framed and submitted to the Committee.

The principle on which the Tables for Flush-decked Steam and Sailing Vessels were prepared was that of allowing a fixed percentage of the total bulk of the vessel above the load-draught as reserve buoyancy; and to render this principle practicable for vessels already built, and for which no accurate drawings were obtainable, the method of employing coefficients of fineness, derived from the registered under-deck tonnage and the principal dimensions, in connexion with the moulded depth, as previously employed by Mr. Martell, was adopted. For spar-decked vessels, the basis was one of strength of construction, and the freeboard arrived at was that which calculations showed would admit of vessels of this type being strained at sea no more than vessels of the same dimensions of the three-decked type.

The basis of the Tables was accepted by the Committee; but, prior to approving the scale of freeboard proposed, the Committee submitted the Tables to the judgment of Shipowners, Ship-builders, and other competent persons throughout the country, and appealed to them for information as to their own experience in the loading of vessels.

In response to the Committee's invitation, a very large amount of valuable information was obtained, and, after the same had been carefully analysed, the Tables were further modified. As amended, they were again laid before the Committee, and, after much deliberation, were finally approved and issued to the public in August, 1882.

The Committee, at the same time, intimated that they were prepared to undertake the duty of assigning suitable freeboards to all types of vessels, classed or unclassed, for record in the Register Book, if requested by the owners to do so, on the basis of the approved Tables, and that each vessel would be dealt with on her merits. To carry their decision into effect, the Committee determined to provide a column in the Register Book for the record of freeboard and moulded depth.

The Tables have now been in operation for some two years, and the measure of their success may be gauged by the fact that during that period the Committee have assigned load-lines to nearly 1,000 vessels, in addition to more than 200 awning-decked vessels which have a fixed load-line as a condition of classification.

CHAPTER XXIII.

IN the autumn of 1882 the important subject of the representation of outports on the Committee of Lloyd's Register again occupied considerable attention. The arrangement then existing, it will be remembered, had been in operation since 1864, when the privilege of being represented on the Committee was first conceded to outports. Under that plan there were fifteen outport members out of a General Committee of forty-one members.

During the interval that had elapsed since the introduction of that arrangement, great changes had taken place in the Mercantile Marine of the country and the relative importance of ports. Some ports which were then comparatively insignificant had acquired great importance, whilst entirely new centres of shipping had also sprung up.

The Committee, therefore, felt that the time had arrived to take into careful consideration the advisability of re-adjusting and enlarging the representation of the outports, in order that the constituent parts of the Committee might be brought into closer accord with the altered conditions of the Mercantile Marine.

Accordingly, a special Sub-Committee was appointed to inquire into the whole subject, and to report thereon to the General Committee, and full statistics bearing on the question were obtained. This Sub-Committee were occupied with the subject for a long time, and after very full deliberation they decided to recommend the General Committee to raise the maximum number of members from forty-one to fifty —the additional members thus created to be distributed amongst the outports.

This proposal came before the General Committee at a special meeting, on the 26th April, 1883, when it was finally adopted. The extension of the representation of outports on the Committee was carried out in such a manner as to preserve as far as practicable the existing relative numbers of Merchants, Shipowners, and Underwriters, in accordance with the original constitution of the Society.

It will be observed, from the particulars given below, that the arrangement of electoral districts is one which practically embraces the whole of the ports in the kingdom. In any case of a district which comprises several ports, the election of the member or members is entrusted to the delegates from local bodies, such as Shipowners' Societies or Chambers of Commerce. Under the latest modifications of the Rules relating to representation on the Committee, the various members are thus apportioned:—

London: Twenty-six members—namely, eight merchants, eight underwriters and eight shipowners, and, in addition, the Chairman of Lloyd's and the

Chairman of the General Shipowners' Society, as *ex-officio* members.

Liverpool: Eight members—namely, four to represent shipowners and four to represent underwriters.

Glasgow: Four members—namely, one to represent shipowners, one merchants, and two underwriters.

The Tyne District: Three members—namely, one to represent shipowners, one merchants, and one underwriters.

Hartlepool, Stockton, and Middlesbro' District: Two members—namely, one to represent shipowners and one underwriters and merchants.

Sunderland: Two members—namely, one to represent shipowners and one underwriters and merchants.

Cardiff, Newport, and Swansea District: One member to represent shipowners and merchants.

Leith, Dundee, and Aberdeen District: One member to represent shipowners and merchants.

Greenock: One member to represent shipowners and merchants.

Hull: One member to represent merchants.

Bristol: One member to represent merchants.

CHAPTER XXIV.

THE Committee have always given a liberal consideration to the circumstances of officers who, from advanced age or other cause, have found themselves unequal to the duties required of them; and provision has been made to enable such officers, on their retirement, to pass their declining years in comfort. Nor has the generosity of the Committee stopped with the officers, but in very many cases it has been extended to the widows and families of officers who have died in the Society's service. This practice was continued until the year 1872, when Rules were adopted requiring all officers who entered the service after that time to assure their lives in the sum of £1,000, the Committee undertaking, on behalf of the Society, to pay a part of the premiums.

Mr. Waymouth, the Secretary, feeling strongly that the operation of the Life Assurance Rules was not satisfactory, and that the absence of a settled scheme for the retirement of officers when incapacitated for the performance of their duties was prejudicial to the true interests of the Society, drew up a Memorandum on the subject, which he brought informally under the notice of some members of the Committee in March, 1883. His representations were favourably entertained, and he was authorised to prepare a scheme embodying his views for the Committee's consideration.

The Committee subsequently gave the subject a very lengthened and careful consideration, and, after various proposals had been discussed, Rules, framed in accordance with Mr. Waymouth's suggestions, providing for the superannuation of the Society's servants, and for the granting of annuities to their widows and orphans, were adopted on the 14th February, 1884, subject to the verification by an actuary of the estimated cost of the operation of the scheme. The accuracy of the estimates submitted to the Committee having been substantially confirmed by an actuary, the Pension Scheme was finally approved, and the regulations relating to life assurance were cancelled at a special meeting of the General Committee on the 7th June, 1884.

According to the Rules adopted by the Committee, every officer in the Society, on attaining the age of 60 years, or earlier if incapacitated by accident or disease, is entitled during the Committee's pleasure to a pension regulated by length of service and amount of salary; and in addition provision is made for annuities according to a definite scale to widows and orphans.

CHAPTER XXV.

THE Society's Register Book has continued to receive such alterations and additions as experience has suggested, and its value to the commercial community as a book of reference has consequently been greatly enhanced. In the volume for 1874 the practice of recording unclassed vessels was revived. As previously stated, the Register Book, as issued in 1834, contained a record of all British ships of 50 tons and above, whether classed or not, but a few years after those unclassed were omitted, and from 1839 till 1874 the Book consisted of classed vessels only.

In the latter year it was determined to include all unclassed vessels of 100 tons and upwards registered in the United Kingdom, and those of large tonnage owned abroad. Then also, for the first time, were introduced useful particulars of the machinery of steamers. Two years later an alphabetical list of the names and addresses of the Owners was added, and this information has been found of much service as a Directory of Managing Shipowners. And so with succeeding years; scarcely one has passed without some addition, more or less im-

portant, having been made to the mass of particulars which make up the Book, the latest being the insertion in the 1883 edition of the particulars of Dry Docks and patent Slipways at all ports throughout the world.

A specimen page of the current edition of the Register Book shown on the opposite side illustrates the vast improvements introduced into the work since 1834, a page of the volume for which year has already been reproduced.

The reports of survey which are being constantly received from the Society's Surveyors all over the world now amount to about 8,000 in a year. These are duly dealt with by a Sub-Committee of Classification who meet twice every week for that purpose. The numerous alterations and additions arising from these surveys are made known to the Subscribers to the Register Book at frequent intervals. In the case of those resident in London, the old practice of posting the books weekly with types is still followed, and a staff of one Superintendent and twenty-two Posters with five Messengers is employed in the Society's office for that purpose. Similar information is conveyed to Subscribers in the Provinces and abroad by means of Supplements issued fortnightly.

As a comparison between 1834 and the present day it may be interesting to state that the number of Subscribers in 1834 was 721, and at the present time is nearly 3,500. The largest vessel classed in the Society's Register Book in 1834 was the ship *George the Fourth*, 1,438 tons, classed 12A1; while the largest in the current issue is the screw-steamer

City of Rome, 8,144 tons, classed 100A1. Moreover, in 1834, comparatively few vessels were above 1,000 tons, and by very far the largest number ranged from 500 tons down to 50 tons; while at the present time there are no less than 195 vessels above 3,000 tons classed in the Society's Register, their collective burthen being 747,470 tons. Of these, 14 vessels are above 5,000 tons, and have a collective tonnage of 78,114 tons; and 62 vessels are above 4,000 tons, and have a collective tonnage of 287,227 tons.

CHAIRMAN.

FROM 1835 TO 1881.

ELLIOTT AND FRY.   BAKER STREET, LONDON, W.

CHAPTER XXVI.

AS already stated, Mr. Thomas Chapman was elected to the office of Chairman in the year 1835. This position he held uninterruptedly from that time until 1881, and it is impossible to over-estimate the value of his services to the Society during this long period. Apart from the excellent judgment he displayed at every conjuncture, his urbanity of manner and conciliatory disposition, combined with the tact with which he guided the deliberations of the Committee, rendered him peculiarly fitted for the important position of Chairman; and to his personal influence, during his long presidency, the Society owes much of its great and continued prosperity.

Upon the occasion of Mr. Chapman's being elected to the office of Chairman for the forty-second time in 1876, the Members of the Committee generally evinced a desire to manifest, in some way that would be gratifying to Mr. Chapman the personal regard and esteem they entertained for him, and also their high appreciation of the distinguished ability

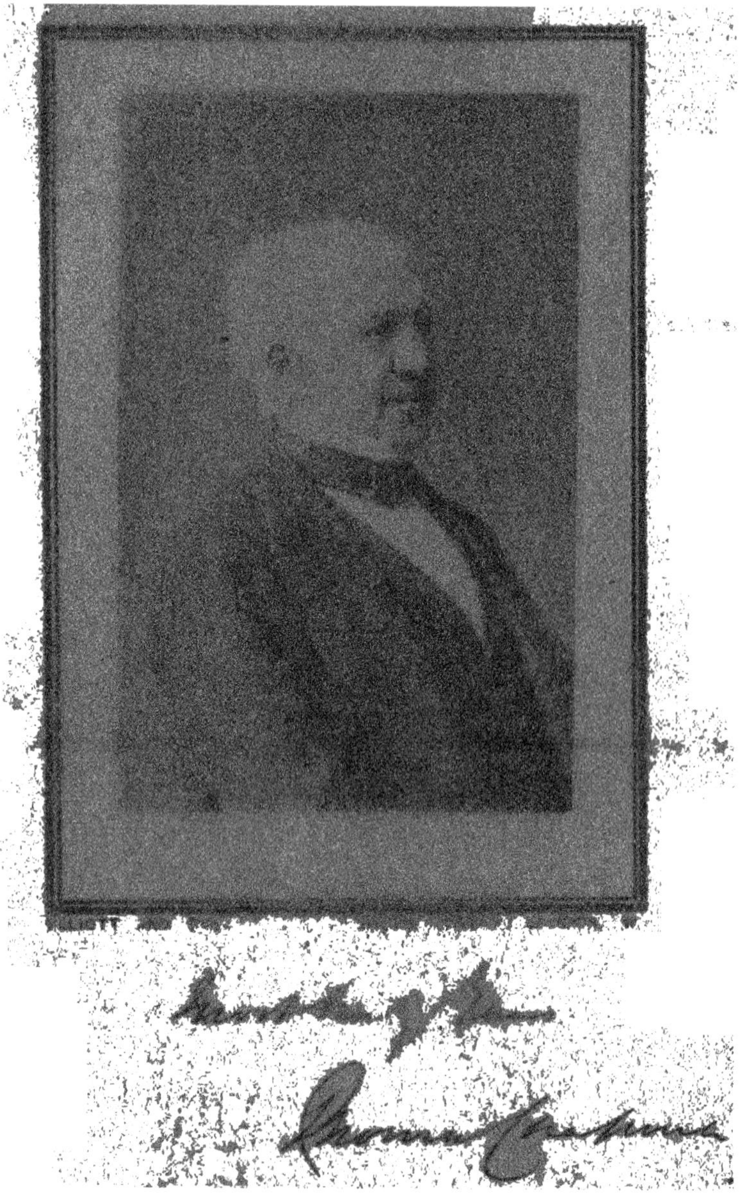

CHAPTER XXVI.

AS already stated, Mr. Thomas Chapman was elected to the office of Chairman in the year 1835. This position he held uninterruptedly from that time until 1881, and it is impossible to over-estimate the value of his services to the Society during this long period. Apart from the excellent judgment he displayed at every conjuncture, his urbanity of manner and conciliatory disposition, combined with the tact with which he guided the deliberations of the Committee, rendered him peculiarly fitted for the important position of Chairman; and to his personal influence, during his long presidency, the Society owes much of its great and continued prosperity.

Upon the occasion of Mr. Chapman's being elected to the office of Chairman for the forty-second time in 1876, the Members of the Committee generally evinced a desire to manifest, in some way that would be gratifying to Mr. Chapman the personal regard and esteem they entertained for him, and also their high appreciation of the distinguished ability with which he had discharged the duties of Chairman, and of the very eminent services rendered by him to the Society and through it to the Mercantile Marine of the country during a period of upwards of forty years. It was therefore determined, in May, 1876, to present to him a piece of plate bearing an appropriate inscription. The presentation was made at a dinner at the Albion Tavern, Aldersgate Street, on Wednesday, the 6th July.

The Right Hon. George J. Goschen, M.P., in proposing the toast of " Prosperity to Lloyd's Register," on that occasion, attributed "the great public confidence placed in the Society to the able manner in which it has been presided over, the singleness of mind with which the Committee and Executive performed their duties, and the integrity of its Surveying staff." A strong feeling had also been shown by the Members that they should subscribe for a portrait of the Chairman, and his consent to sit for it having been obtained, Mr. E. J. Gregory, A.R.A., was chosen to execute the painting, which now adorns the Board-room in the Society's office.

The presentation made by the Committee offered a fitting occasion to the Surveying staff to give an expression of their own regard for the Chairman, and a suggestion to this effect having been made by the Chief Surveyor to his colleagues, it was received by them with hearty approval, and the whole staff of the Society's Surveyors at home and abroad combined to mark their esteem for the Chairman. The clerical staff of the Society, animated with like feelings, also determined to ask his acceptance of a testimonial at their hands. On the 5th of October, 1876, these presentations were made, and the Chairman, in accepting the same, gave an interesting account of the Society's career during the long period of upwards of forty years that he had presided over it.

Mr. Chapman continued to fill the office of Chairman until 1881, when the claims of advancing years induced him to retire, after rendering about forty-seven years of most excellent service to the Society and to the Mercantile Marine of the country.

On Mr. Chapman's retirement, Mr. W. H. Tindall, son of the late Mr. W. Tindall, who was so prominent a Member of the Committee at the formation of the Society, was elected to the office of Chairman.

Mr. W. H. Tindall had been a Member of the Committee since 1856, and had acted for eleven years as Deputy-Chairman, in which office he was succeeded by Mr. Michael Wills, a member of twenty-one years' standing.

Mr. Tindall and Mr. Wills still occupy the above-named offices, while that of Chairman of the Sub-Committees of Classification is filled by Mr. T. B. Walker, who has presided over these Committees since the year 1870, and has been a member of the General Committee during twenty years.

The following is a list of the Chairmen, Deputy-Chairmen, and Chairmen of the Sub-Committees of Classification since the formation of the Society in

1834; also the periods during which they respectively filled their several offices:—

	NAMES.	FROM	UNTIL
Chairmen	D. Carruthers	1834	1835
	T. Chapman, F.R.S., F.S.A.	1835	1881
	W. H. Tindall	1881	present time.
Deputy-Chairmen	Crawford D. Kerr	1834	1835
	H. Blanchard	1835	1838
	William Tindall	1838	1853
	S. Ellerby	1853	1857
	Duncan Dunbar	1857	1861
	George Marshall	1861	1871
	W. H. Tindall	1871	1881
	Michael Wills	1881	present time.
Chairmen of Committees of Classification.	John Robinson	1834	1860
	W. C. Harnett, F.S.A.	1860	1870
	T. B. Walker	1870	present time.

In looking down the list of gentlemen who have sat upon the Committee during the past fifty years, we see many names which occur year after year. For instance, Mr. George Allfrey, Mr. George Hanson, and Mr. John Robinson, who were members of the Provisional Committee in 1834, continued to serve for thirty-six, twenty-seven, and twenty-six years respectively. Of the Permanent Committee, whose names appear in the Register Book for the year 1835, Mr. William Tindall, Mr. George Whitmore, and Mr. George F. Young, M.P., were also members during eighteen, twenty-six, and thirty-two years respectively. As seen by the above list, Mr. Tindall was Deputy-Chairman during fifteen years of the time that he served upon the Committee.

With other names, too, there occur those of Mr. W. Harnett, F.S.A., who sat from 1839 until 1870, during ten years of which he was Chairman of the Classification Sub-Committee; Mr. G. Fenning, who was a member during thirty-five years; Mr. G. Hankey, who sat for a period of thirty years; and Mr. W. Wilson Saunders, F.R.S., whose term of membership extended to thirty-two years. Besides the above, other prominent names occur, such as those of Mr. Duncan Dunbar and Mr. George Marshall, both of whom occupied the office of Deputy-Chairman.

Amongst the earliest officers of the Society, we find the name of Mr. Nathaniel Symonds, who acted as Secretary to the Committee until January, 1837, when he was succeeded by Mr. Charles Graham, who had previously been in the service of the Lords Commissioners of the Admiralty. Soon after Mr. Symonds's appointment followed that of Mr. Henry Adams, who had in 1815 entered the service of the Register known as the Green Book, and who still (1884) occupies the position of Chief Clerk in this Society's office,—forming a living link between the Association which took its rise in the middle of last century and the present Society. Somewhat later Mr. George B. Seyfang (the late Secretary) was elected, he having been in the employ of the Society known as the Red Book for some years previously. The Superintendent of the posting of the Register Book and one or two of the Posters appear also to have been taken from the staff of the latter Registry.

Mr. George Bayley was the earliest of the Society's principal Surveyors, and he continued to serve the Committee in that office from his appointment in 1834 until his resignation in 1844, when the Committee determined that it was essential to the efficient control and superintendence of the Surveyors' department that a principal Surveyor should be appointed of high qualification. The gentleman selected by the Committee was Mr. A. F. B. Creuze, F.R.S., who continued to occupy the position until his death in November, 1852. Mr. Creuze was a member of the first Royal School of Naval Architecture, and was associated with Messrs. Chatfield & Read, members of the same school, in the preparation of successful competitive designs for ships of war, and in writing a most able and comprehensive Report to the Admiralty upon Naval Construction. Mr. Creuze was also the author of a separate treatise on Naval Architecture, published in the seventh edition of the "Encyclopædia Britannica." While he was in the service of the Society, an application was received from the Admiralty, and granted by the Committee, for permission to be given to him to design a frigate for the Royal Navy. Mr. Creuze was also one of the judges appointed to decide upon the merits of the several improvements in naval architecture which were shown in the Great Exhibition of 1851.

It may here be remarked that in May, 1855, the services of Mr. Graham, who had been Secretary since

1837, were unfortunately lost to the Committee through the death of that gentleman ; and he was succeeded in his office by Mr. George B. Seyfang, who had been a Clerk in the London office of the Society. Mr. Seyfang was an able Secretary, and continued to fill this important and responsible office until his death, which occurred in 1872.

After the death of Mr. Creuze, the office of Chief Surveyor was jointly filled by Messrs. J. Martin and J. H. Ritchie. Mr. Martin entered the service of the Society in 1841, having previously been trained in Her Majesty's Dockyard at Chatham ; and Mr. Ritchie, who had been in business as a shipbuilder, was elected in 1842.

The preparation of the Rules for the Construction of Iron Ships in 1854, and the revisions and amplifications of those Rules in 1863, were made under the direction of these gentlemen, assisted, as they were, by an able staff of Surveyors, both in London and the outports. Much credit is due to them for their compilation of these early Rules, which had to be framed on practical experience and information collected from reports received from the Society's Surveyors.

So highly were the Society's two principal Surveyors esteemed by their professional brethren, that, in the address delivered at the opening of the Institution of Naval Architects, in the year 1860, they were referred to in the following terms :—" The principal Surveyors to Lloyd's famous Register Offices are likewise known to be gentlemen of marked ability and most ample experience, and they also are with us."

They were at the same time elected as Members

of Council; while Mr. Chapman, the Chairman, and Mr. Duncan Dunbar, the Deputy-Chairman, were elected as Vice-Presidents of the Institution.

Messrs. Martin and Ritchie were the Society's principal Surveyors until the year 1870, when Mr. Waymouth was associated with them in the performance of their official duties. Mr. Ritchie retired in 1871 and Mr. Martin the following year, each gentleman being granted a pension by the Committee. Upon their retirement, the duties of their office remained under the sole charge of Mr. Waymouth.

On the death of Mr. G. B. Seyfang, in 1872, Mr. Waymouth was appointed Secretary, and was succeeded as Chief Surveyor by Mr. Martell, whose office has grown in importance and responsibility with the expansion of the Society that has taken place during the last ten years. At the same time the office of Assistant-Secretary was created, and conferred upon Mr. R. Gillespie, who had been in the service of the Society as a Clerk since the year 1839.

Another addition to the staff was made in 1874, when Mr. Parker was selected by the Committee to be the head of the engineering department, which was instituted in that year.

As instances of the confidence which has been placed by the Government of the country in the Society and its officials, the following facts may be cited:—

As already stated, the Committee in 1848, at the instance of the Lords Commissioners of the Admiralty, authorized Mr. Creuze, then the Society's Chief Surveyor, to design a large frigate for the Royal Navy;

and in 1865, upon a question being raised in Parliament as to the strength of H.M.S. *Royal Alfred*, then in process of conversion into an armour-plated block ship, the matter was, upon special application from the Admiralty, referred to Mr. Martin and Mr. Waymouth, two of the Society's principal Surveyors at that time.

In the year 1871, Mr. Thos. Chapman, the Chairman, served upon the Royal Commission appointed to take evidence and report upon the circumstances leading to the loss of H.M.S. *Megæra*. In 1873 Mr. George Duncan, a member of the Committee, sat upon the Royal Commission relating to Unseaworthy Ships; and in 1876 Mr. Duncan and Mr. William Young, another member of the Committee, were two of the Royal Commissioners on the Inquiry into the Spontaneous Combustion of Coal in Ships.

Upon the invitation of the Lords Commissioners of the Admiralty, Mr. B. Waymouth, the Secretary, in 1880, served upon a Committee to inquire into the circumstances relating to the loss of H.M.S. *Atalanta*; and later in the same year, Mr. John Glover, a member of the General Committee, Mr. T. B. Royden, a member of the Liverpool Committee, and Mr. Waymouth, were three of the Royal Commissioners appointed to report upon the operation of the Tonnage Laws.

At the present time Mr. James Laing and Mr. William Gray, members of the General Committee, Mr. T. B. Royden, of the Liverpool Committee, and Mr. B. Martell, the Society's Chief Surveyor, are serving upon the Departmental Committee appointed by the Board of Trade to investigate and report in regard to the question of fixing a proper Load-line for Merchant Ships; whilst in the Royal Commission, which has just been appointed to inquire into the Loss of Life at Sea, we find the names of Messrs. Henry Green, James McGregor, L. C. Wakefield, and John Warrack, all members of the General Committee, and Mr. T. B. Royden, of the Liverpool Committee of the Society.

CHAPTER XXVII.

AND now, in bringing to a conclusion this short account of the rise and progress of LLOYD'S REGISTER OF BRITISH AND FOREIGN SHIPPING, it remains but to glance briefly at the position which the Society at present occupies in the estimation of the public.

That the growth of the Society's business has been co-extensive with the perfecting and extending of its organisation will be evident when it is stated that the Shipping built under the Society's inspection in the United Kingdom and elsewhere during the last few years amounts to :—

<pre>
In 1879, 501 vessels of 521,338 tons.
 „ 1880, 480   ..   517,664 „
 „ 1881, 582   757,802 „
 „ 1882, 682   ,,   989,002 „
 „ 1883, 848   „   1,116,555 „
</pre>

While out of the total number of merchant vessels built in the United Kingdom during the same period, including those of every type and nationality, about

90 per cent. have, on the average, been surveyed and classed by the Society.

The extent of the Society's progress is indicated not alone by the large amount of shipping which comes under its inspection, but also by the performance of new duties and the assumption of new responsibilities, such as have marked the later years of the Society's existence.

When constituted on its present basis in 1834, the Society concerned itself only with the Survey of Shipping within the limits of the United Kingdom, and had only sixty-three Surveyors. It has from time to time made one addition after another, until now its staff of Surveyors numbers one hundred and seventy-five, and its ramifications have been extended to most of the important ports in both hemispheres, and may be said to encircle the globe.

While growing in extent, its duties have also increased in complexity with the spread of scientific knowledge, and there is now comprised within its sphere of operations a great variety of duties, each calling for the exercise of the highest skill and of special training.

For instance, in addition to the Survey and Classification of Wood, Iron, Steel, and Composite Vessels,—perfected from time to time as experience suggested,—the Society now carries on the Inspection during and after construction of Engines and Boilers of Steam Vessels by a large staff of experienced Marine Engineers;—it controls and regulates the testing of Anchors and Chains at eight out of the nine principal Proving-houses in the country, under the provisions of the Chain and Anchors Act of 1871 ;—it undertakes the testing of Steel intended to be used in the construction of Ships and Boilers, and performs a like duty in the Inspection of large Ship and Engine Forgings and Castings ;—it provides for the Survey and Classification, under Special Rules, of Yachts, and also of Vessels built for particular purposes ;—while the most recent, and one of the most important, instances of the development of the Society's responsibilities is to be found in the promulgation by the Committee, two years ago, of Freeboard Tables, by which the Society undertakes to assign maximum Load-lines to Vessels of all types.

While much depends upon the Committee as the governing and directing body, their labour would be of little avail if they had not able and intelligent officers to give effect to their instructions. The Society's staff of surveyors, strengthened as it has been from time to time by the appointment of men possessed of high scientific culture and wide practical experience, comprises a body of officers whose collective knowledge and experience in all that pertains to Naval Architecture and Marine Engineering, it is universally admitted, it would be difficult to equal; and, by transferring the Surveyors occasionally from one part of the country to another, such a uniformity of practice at the several ports is attained as cannot fail to be advantageous to all concerned.

The Society, founded upon voluntary principles, and deriving its strength, not from legislative enactment, but from the confidence which it inspires in the Shipping and Mercantile community, has gone on from year to year growing with the growth and strengthening with the strength of the Mercantile Marine. During the last ten years of its existence it has progressed by leaps and bounds, until at the present moment it can claim to be a thoroughly Representative and truly International Registry of Merchant Shipping.

COMMITTEE OF MANAGEMENT.

COMMITTEE OF MANAGEMENT.

1884-85.

William Henry Tindall, *Chairman.*
Michael Wills, *Deputy-Chairman.*
Thomas B. Walker, *Chairman of the Sub-Committees of Classification.*

MEMBERS ELECTED IN LONDON.

H. J. Bristow,
John Corry,
Solomon I. DaCosta,
James Dixon,
George Duncan,
John Glover,
Henry Green,
George Lidgett,
H. E. Montgomerie,
Frederic B. B. Natusch,
Henry Nixon,
James Park,
A. O. Robinson,
Wm. Frederick Saunders,
Charles R. Tatham,
John Henry Tod,
George Dorman Tyser,
Leonard C. Wakefield,
Arthur Oates Wilkinson,
John Willis,
William Young.

Rt. Hon. George J. Goschen, M.P., *Chairman of the Committee of Lloyd's.*
William Strang, *Chairman of the General Shipowners' Society.*

MEMBERS ELECTED AT THE PRINCIPAL OUTPORTS.

FOR LIVERPOOL:

H. T. Wallace, *Chairman of the Liverpool Committee.*
J. H. Worthington, *Deputy-Chairman ditto.*
John S. Allen,
Donald Kennedy,
John Rankin,
Thomas R. Shallcross,
C. B. Vallance,
John Williamson.

GLASGOW { William Adamson, Walter Easton, Thomas Low, James McGregor.
SUNDERLAND { Ralph M. Hudson, James Laing.
HARTLEPOOL DISTRICT { William Gray, John Hall.
BRISTOL—John Evans.

LEITH DISTRICT—John Warrack.
GREENOCK—Dugald Macdougall.
TYNE DISTRICT { R. S. Donkin, J. D. Milburn, E. H. Watts.
CARDIFF DISTRICT } Col. E. S. Hill, C.B.
HULL—Henry J. Atkinson.

TRUSTEES.

George Allfrey,
George Duncan,
William Henry Tindall,
John Henry Tod,
Thomas B. Walker,
Michael Wills.

SECRETARY.— Bernard Waymouth.

ASSISTANT-SECRETARY.—Richard Gillespie.

LIVERPOOL BRANCH.

COMMITTEE.

H. T. Wallace, *Chairman.*

J. H. Worthington, *Deputy-Chairman.*

John S. Allen,	James Poole,
Samuel Cross,	John Rankin,
David Fernie,	Thomas R. Shallcross,
Donald Kennedy,	C. B. Vallance,
Henry Lenton,	John Williamson.

Thomas B. Royden, *Chairman of the Shipbuilders' Association* (*ex officio*).

SECRETARY—John Frederick Light.

LIST OF SURVEYORS.

The SURVEYORS *at the following* PORTS *are exclusively the Officers of the Society, and are not permitted to engage in any other business or employment whatsoever.*

LONDON.

Benjamin Martell, *Chief Surveyor.*
Harry J. Cornish, } *Assistants to Chief*
Thomas Edwards, } *Surveyor.*
William Parker, { *Chief Engineer Surveyor.*
James T. Milton, } *Assistants to Chief*
David Purves, } *Engineer Surveyor.*

William C. Davey.
Senhouse Martindale.
John W. Miles.
James H. Truscott.
Thomas C. Read.
Philip Jenkins.
Edward C. Champness.
E. J. Tierney.
Thomas S. Warren.
J. T. Roberts.
George R. Mares.
H. Hand.

Engineer Surveyors { George E. Wilkinson.
Charles E. Stromeyer.

ABERDEEN	Thomas W. Kettle.
ABERYSTWITH	William John.
BANGOR	Thomas Devonald.
BARROW and WHITEHAVEN	{ John Lawrence. Charles Buchanan.
Engineer Surveyor	Duncan Ritchie.
BELFAST	James Turpin.
BIDEFORD	Charles Fittock.
BRISTOL	H. M. Williams.
CARDIFF and NEWPORT	{ Henry T. Tyrrell. J. G. G. Rule.
Ship and Engineer Surveyors ...	{ A. E. Keydell. George Kendall.
DUBLIN	John Mugford.
DUNDEE	George P. Cooper.
Engineer Surveyor	John Sturrock.
FALMOUTH	William Bowden.
Engineer Surveyor	Lawrence Moreton.
GLASGOW	{ William T. Mumford. Thomas J. Dodd. George Stanbury. Thomas J. House. Charles Fowling. Charles Edwards. Charles E. Burney. Herbert W. Dove. William Andrews.

List of Surveyors.

Engineer Surveyors	{ James Mollison. { Walter E. Robson.
Ship and Engineer Surveyors ...	{ G. L. Hindmarsh. { John Sanderson.
Inspector of Forgings	George Newcomb.
GREENOCK	{ Christopher Besant. { John Dawkins. { S. J. P. Thearle.
Engineer Surveyor	Andrew C. Heron.
HARTLEPOOL	{ Charles Davidson. { Frederick W. Bonniwell. { Thomas Phillips. { Joseph Thomson.
Engineer Surveyors	{ James Bain. { James Sankey.
HULL	James McNeil.
Engineer Surveyor	John B. Stevens.
LEITH	William Paulsen.
Ship and Engineer Surveyor ...	William J. Darling.
LIVERPOOL	{ John F. Light. { Edward C. Wheeler. { William Moverly. { Charles Skentelbery.
Engineer Surveyors	{ Peter McGregor. { J. E. Stoddart.
MILFORD HAVEN	James D. Warlow.
NEWCASTLE	{ Henry J. Boolds. { James Sibun. { Thomas H. Cooke. { Thomas Shilston. { J. W. Scullard. { Robert Williamson.
Engineer Surveyors	{ John Brockat. { J. F. Walliker. { Richard Hirst.
Ship and Engineer Surveyors ...	{ R. W. Coomber. { John H. Heck.
PLYMOUTH	Edward Elliott.
QUEENSTOWN	J. T. Head.
SOUTHAMPTON	James L. Sinnette.
SUNDERLAND	{ Richard J. Reed. { Joseph Keen. { William Bath. { Jesse Williams. { William Johnstone. { T. H. Sandry.
Engineer Surveyors	{ William Allison. { Patrick Salmon. { G. A. Milner.
Inspector of Forgings	Henry Cameron.

SWANSEA ... ... Thomas Ashton.

The SURVEYORS *at the following* PORTS *do not hold appointments as the exclusive Servants of the Society.*

GUERNSEY ... ... George T. Sullock.
IPSWICH ... ... William Taylor.
LYNN ... ... William F. Beaumont.
ORKNEYS ... ... James Mowat.
PENZANCE ... ... Hugh Tregarthen.
RAMSGATE ... ... Edward Jones.
SLIGO ... ... William Pollexfen.
WATERFORD ... ... Andrew Horn.
WEXFORD ... ... Robert Sparrow.

COLONIAL AND FOREIGN SURVEYORS.

France.
BORDEAUX ... ... Jules Vandercruyce.
  Engineer Surveyor ... ... A. Donzelle.
HAVRE, *Ship and Engineer Surveyor* A. Le Laidler.
MARSEILLES, *Ship and Engineer Surveyor*... ... ... } Francis Westerman.
NANTES ... ... Auguste L. Guibert.

Belgium.
BELGIUM ... ... Heinrich Paasch.
  Engineer Surveyor ... ... Francis Demblon.

Holland.
AMSTERDAM ... ... D. D. Borchers.
  Exclusive Engineer Surveyor ... W. F. D. van Ollefen.
ROTTERDAM ... ... Jan C. W. Loos.
VEENDAM ... ... H. P. Hazewinkel.

Germany.
HAMBURG ... ... Emil Padderatz.
  Engineer Surveyor ... ... J. A. Libbertz.
  Assistant Surveyor at ROSTOCK ... W. Cordes.
  Assistant Ship and Engineer Surveyor at BREMERHAVEN ... } F. H. T. Thomsen.

Denmark.
COPENHAGEN, *Ship and Engineer Surveyor* ... ... } P. Fred. Kindler.

Norway.
BERGEN, *Ship and Engineer Surveyor* ... E. Hougland.

Sweden.

GOTHENBURG, *Ship and Engineer Surveyor* ... Carl Axel Möller.

Spain and Portugal.

BARCELONA, *Ship and Engineer Surveyor* ... J. J. Browne.
BILBAO ... J. T. de Ugarte.
CADIZ, *Ship and Engineer Surveyor* ... James Cochrane.
LISBON, *Ship and Engineer Surveyor* ... J. Westwood.

Italy and Austria.

GENOA ... Francesco Schiaffino.
   Engineer Surveyor ... Francis Westerman.
LEGHORN ... Costantino Gori.
TRIESTE ... Elias Florio.
   Engineer Surveyor ... Frederic Schnabl.
   Assistant Surveyor at FIUME ... Ignazio Bonetich.
   Ditto at VENICE ... Matteo Fabro.
   Ditto at LUSSINO ... Antonio E. Tarrabocchia.

Malta.

MALTA, *Ship and Engineer Surveyor* W. Hinchcliffe.

Russia.

SEBASTOPOL, *Ship and Engineer Surveyor* ... John E. Corry.

British North America.

PRINCE EDWARD ISLAND ... Richard Sloggett.
QUEBEC ... John Dick.
ST. JOHN ... Charles R. Coker.

United States.

NEW YORK, *Principal Surveyor for the United States—Exclusive Surveyor* } Thomas Congdon.
BALTIMORE ... Edward H. Sanford.
   Engineer Surveyor ... Richard Wells.
BOSTON, *Ship and Engineer Surveyor* ... Oliver L. Shaw.
PHILADELPHIA, *Ship and Engineer Surveyor* ... John Haug.

British Guiana.

DEMERARA ... Alexander Duncan.

South Africa.

CAPE TOWN ... James Anderson.
PORT NATAL ... Alexander Airth.

East Indies.

BOMBAY	A. C. Clarke.
Engineer Surveyor	James Moir.
CALCUTTA	D. McKellar.
MAURITIUS	John Cowin.
SINGAPORE	Charles Fittock.
Engineer Surveyor	Robert Park.

Java.

BATAVIA, *Ship and Engineer Surveyor*	William Fargie.
Assist. Ship Surveyor at CHERIBON	M. Priebee.
SAMARANG	A. J. Herckenrath.
SOURABAYA	P. Vader.

Philippine Islands.

MANILA, *Ship and Engineer Surveyor*...	Frederick H. Sawyer.

China.

HONG KONG	Edward Burnie.
Engineer Surveyor	Andrew Johnston.
SHANGHAI	C. G. Warburg.
Engineer Surveyor	H. Sonne.

Australia, Tasmania, and New Zealand.

ADELAIDE	William Begg.
MELBOURNE	Douglas Elder.
SYDNEY	Robert F. Pockley.
BRISBANE	William B. Brown.
HOBART (Tasmania)	Donald Macmillan.
AUCKLAND, N.Z.	M. T. Clayton.
CHRISTCHURCH, N.Z.	William Watson.
DUNEDIN, N.Z.	James Ure Russell.
WELLINGTON, N.Z.	William Bendall.

FINIS

WYMAN AND SONS, PRINTERS, GREAT QUEEN STREET, LONDON, W.C.

374863

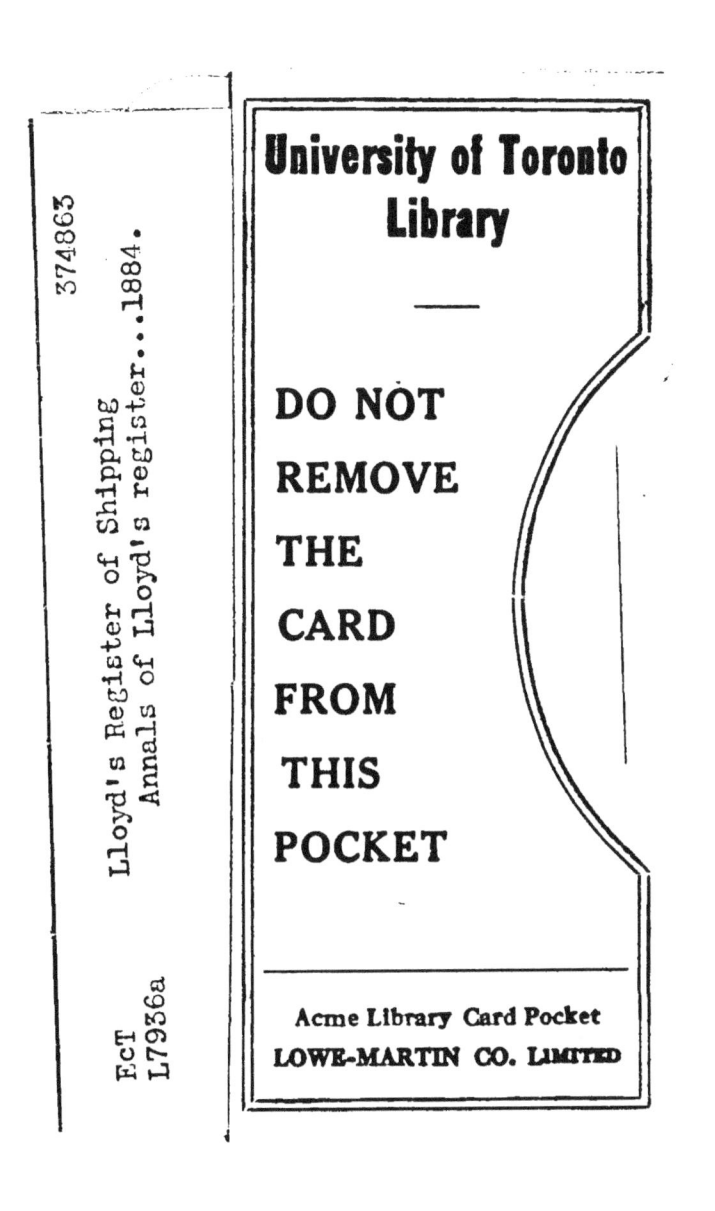

Lloyd's Register of Shipping
Annals of Lloyd's register...1884.

EcT
L7936a

University of Toronto Library

DO NOT
REMOVE
THE
CARD
FROM
THIS
POCKET

Acme Library Card Pocket
LOWE-MARTIN CO. LIMITED

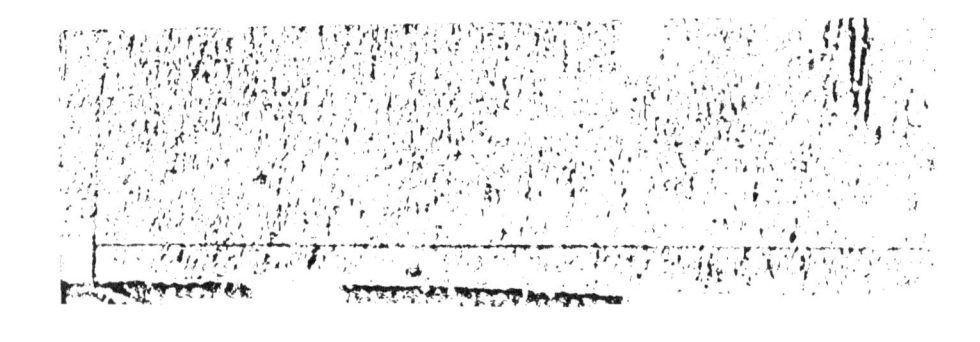